THE EASY
ELITE GOURMET
AIR FRYER
COOKBOOK

EASY, FLAVORFUL AIR FRYER RECIPES TO

LIVE A LIGHTER LIFE

TONY JACKSON

CONTENTS

INTRODUCTION

How do Elite Gourmet Air Fryer Works?

Air fryers work by circulating hot air around the food in a very similar way to convection ovens. A heating element inside the air fryer distributes hot air through a fan so that it's pushed around the food in circular motions. This way of cooking food is actually quicker than traditional methods because the heat is evenly distributed around the food. If you're cooking frozen fries in an air fryer, you can expect this to take around 15 minutes.

While air-frying might not be quite as fast as deep-frying, you'll be using significantly less oil, and you won't need to blot your food onto a paper kitchen towel. Most air fryers have removable baskets in which you place your food, and these have small holes all around their edges that allow the hot air to reach the food inside. In order for the air to circulate effectively though, you'll need to make sure you're not overfilling the basket so that the hot air can reach all sides of the food. Air fryer baskets sit pretty snugly against the sides of the appliance, ensuring that minimal heat is lost during cooking.

What Are the Benefits of Elite Gourmet Air Fryer?

I'm sure you have seen the online buzz about air fryers! These appliances are definitely the most popular and trendy thing happening in the kitchen this year. Maybe you are curious about what all the hype is about? When I first heard about them, I was curious as well. Why ARE people so excited about these things? I love some good fries as much as the next person, but can one unit really do more than that? How can frying anything be healthy?

These appliances are not a fryer in the same way that a deep-fat fryer is. They are more like a small, self-contained convection oven. They use electrical elements to quickly heat the air, and then circulate this hot air around and through your food. This hot air cooks the food quickly, so crispy things get browned but the inside stays moist and delicious. Here are some benefits of cooking with an air fryer:

1. Healthier Cooking

So, how can frying something be healthy? Easy! These appliances can be used without any oil at all, or with just a tiny spritz of oil if you choose to use it. You can cook frozen fries, onion rings, wings and more, and still get really crispy results without the extra oil. Compared to using my oven, the fries from the air fryer were crispier but not dried out, and using it to make breaded zucchini wedges was even more impressive!

2. Quicker Meals

Since they are smaller than an oven and circulate the air around with fans, they cook foods faster as well. An oven can take up to 20-30 minutes to properly preheat, whereas these fryers come to the temperature within minutes. I was really impressed that my frozen fries were perfect after 15 minutes when they take up to 45 minutes in the oven. If you need to make snacks or meals in a hurry, you will probably love this time saver.

3. Versatility

I think this is my favorite feature of an air fryer. You can do SO MUCH with it! Yes, it fries really well compared to an oven. But it also can bake (even cakes), broil, roast, grill and stir fry! Feel like chicken and snow peas for dinner? Easy to make with one of these.

You can cook fresh and frozen foods and even reheat leftovers in them. I have done meats, fish, casseroles, sandwiches and a lot of different veggies in mine. Some fryers come with extra features, like a rotisserie rack, grill pan or elevated cooking rack. Dividable baskets mean you can cook several things at the same time as well. It is impressive that a single unit can cook so many things in so many ways.

Depending on the size of your fryer, there are a lot of different accessories you can buy. Cake and pizza pans, kabob skewers and steamer inserts are just a few of the accessories I have seen available. There are many recipe books for sale, and online recipes are easy to find too.

4. Space Saver

If you have a small kitchen, or live in a dorm room or shared housing, you might appreciate this benefit. Most of these units are about the size of a coffee maker. They don't take up too much room on the counter, and they are usually easy to store away or move. I appreciate the fact that they can replace other appliances like a toaster oven, and some folks use them in kitchenettes or RVs that lack a real oven. They are very handy to have in an office break room too!

5. Ease of Use

Most fryers are really easy to use- just select the temperature and the cooking time, add food and shake a few times while cooking. No need to fuss or stir like using the stove top.

The baskets make shaking your food simple and fast as well, and the unit doesn't lose a lot of heat when you open it. So feel free to peek while cooking if you want! Unlike an oven, you won't be slowing things down if you do.

6. Ease of Clean Up

One part of cooking that most of us don't enjoy is the clean up. With an air fryer, you just have a basket and pan to clean, and many are even dishwasher safe. With non-stick coated parts, food usually isn't stuck to the pan and instead slides right off onto your plate. It takes just a few minutes to wash up after using. This inspires me to cook at home more often because I don't dread the clean up!

7. Energy Efficiency

These fryers are more efficient that using an oven, and they won't heat up you house either. I've been using mine during a heat wave, and I love that my kitchen isn't hot while I'm using it. If you are trying to keep your house cool during the summer, or are worried about your electric bill, then you will be impressed with how efficient these units are.

How to Use Elite Gourmet Air Fryer?

Here are a few more tips for getting the most out of your air fryer:

1. Adjust the Cooking Temperature

When converting a recipe with a suggested temperature for deep-frying or cooking in a traditional oven, lower the air fryer's temperature by 25°F to achieve similar results. So if a recipe calls for deep-frying chicken in oil heated to 350°F, air fry at 325°F. The same rule applies for converting roasting recipes. This adjustment is needed because the circulating air makes the heat of the cooking environment more consistent, and thus more intense than traditional cooking methods. Remember to pre-heat your air fryer to temperature—it usually takes less than 5 minutes—before filling the basket, just as you would with any other cooking method.

2. Toss Ingredients With Oil, Sparingly

In general, you should toss food with one to two tablespoons of oil (whichever kind you like: olive, coconut, canola). Foods that are naturally fattier, like meatballs, needn't be tossed in any additional oil. For foods that have been battered or dredged in flour, we recommend spraying the air fryer basket or rack first with cooking spray, laying your battered or dredged food in the basket or rack in a single layer, and then giving the food a light spritz of cooking spray just to coat the top. That little bit of oil is essential for getting foods to turn golden-brown, crisp, and appealing.

3. Fill the Air Fryer Basket or Rack

Battered and floured foods should be placed in one layer in an air fryer basket or rack. Some models offer racks that allow for two layers—if yours does, feel free to double up. For things like French fries or "roasted" vegetables, you can load the air fryer basket to the top; however, a fuller basket will require a longer cooking time and will result in food that's not quite as crisp as a basket with a smaller amount of food. It's also a good idea to give full baskets a shake every 3 to 5 minutes to make sure food is cooking evenly—many models will pause the timer when you open the drawer, expressly for this purpose.

4. Check for Doneness Early

Again, because the circulating air helps the air-fryer cooking environment maintain a more consistent temperature than other cooking methods, foods tend to cook faster in an air fryer than they do when being deep-fried or cooked in a conventional oven. That means if you're converting a recipe you already know and love to one cooked in an air fryer, you'll want to check the food about two-thirds of the way through the suggested cooking time to test doneness. Those fish sticks say they'll be done in 15 minutes? Check them at 10 minutes.

5. Make French Fries as Often as Possible

We know why you're really thinking about buying that air fryer, so here it is: yup, frozen French fries can be put right into the air fryer, no oil necessary, and cooked at 350°F for about 15 minutes. Be sure to give them a shake or a toss once or twice during cooking. Fresh-cut fries should first be soaked in hot water for at least 10 minutes (30 minutes is better) to remove excess starch. After soaking, drain and dry fries with a kitchen towel, toss in 1 to 2 tablespoons vegetable oil, then air fry at 350°F for about 20 minutes, again shaking once or twice during cooking. And in either case, don't forget to salt them when they're finished cooking.

How to Clean and Care for Elite Gourmet Air Fryer?

Traditionally, deep frying food is very messy. You end up with a lot of dirty pans, grimy utensils, and a greasy coating on everything around the fryer. Air fryers, on the other hand, are relatively clean. The cooking basket is completely enclosed, which eliminates splattering and all the fat, grease, and oil in your food drips down into the oil pan below. This doesn't mean there's no need to clean, however. Your air fryer should be cleaned every time you use it.

➢ **To clean your Elite Gourmet air fryer:**

✧ Unplug the air fryer from the wall socket and let it cool down.

✧ Wipe the outside with a damp cloth.

✧ Wash the pan, tray, and basket with hot water and dishwashing soap. All the air fryer's removable components are dishwasher safe, so they can be placed in a dishwasher if you would prefer not to wash them by hand.

✧ Clean in the inside of the air fryer with hot water and a cloth or sponge.

✧ If there is any food stuck to the heating element above the food basket, clean it off with a brush.

✧ Make sure the pan, tray, and basket are completely dry before putting them back into the air fryer.

➢ **To care your Elite Gourmet air fryer:**

Beyond regularly cleanings, your air fryer requires some basic maintenance to make sure that it doesn't get damaged or start functioning incorrectly. This includes:

✧ Inspecting the cords before each use. Never plug a damaged or frayed cord into an outlet. It can cause serious injury or even death. Make sure the cords are clean and damage-free before using your air fryer.

✧ Making sure the unit is clean and free of any debris before you start cooking. If it has been a long time since you last used your air fryer, check inside. Some dust may have accumulated. If there is any food residue on the basket for pan, clean it out before you start cooking.

✧ Make sure the air fryer is placed upright, on a level surface, before you start cooking.

✧ Make sure the air fryer is not placed close to a wall or another appliance. Air fryers need at least 4 inches of space behind them and 4 inches of space above them in order to adequately vent steam and hot air while cooking. Placing them in an enclosed space may cause the fryer to overheat.

✧ Visually inspect each component, including the basket, pan and handle prior to each use. If you find any damaged components, contact the manufacturer and get them replaced.

Poultry Recipes

Honey Lemon Thyme Glazed Cornish Hen

Servings: 2

Cooking Time: 20 Minutes

Ingredients:

- 1 (2-pound) Cornish game hen, split in half
- olive oil
- salt and freshly ground black pepper
- ¼ teaspoon dried thyme
- ¼ cup honey
- 1 tablespoon lemon zest
- juice of 1 lemon
- 1½ teaspoons chopped fresh thyme leaves
- ½ teaspoon soy sauce
- freshly ground black pepper

Directions:

1. Split the game hen in half by cutting down each side of the backbone and then cutting through the breast. Brush or spray both halves of the game hen with the olive oil and then season with the salt, pepper and dried thyme.

2. Preheat the air fryer to 390°F.

3. Place the game hen, skin side down, into the air fryer and air-fry for 5 minutes. Turn the hen halves over and air-fry for 10 minutes.

4. While the hen is cooking, combine the honey, lemon zest and juice, fresh thyme, soy sauce and pepper in a small bowl.

5. When the air fryer timer rings, brush the honey glaze onto the game hen and continue to air-fry for another 3 to 5 minutes, just until the hen is nicely glazed, browned and has an internal temperature of 165°F.

6. Let the hen rest for 5 minutes and serve warm.

Crispy Duck With Cherry Sauce

Servings: 2   Cooking Time: 33 Minutes

Ingredients:

- 1 whole duck (up to 5 pounds), split in half, back and rib bones removed
- 1 teaspoon olive oil
- salt and freshly ground black pepper
- Cherry Sauce:
- 1 tablespoon butter
- 1 shallot, minced
- ½ cup sherry
- ¾ cup cherry preserves 1 cup chicken stock
- 1 teaspoon white wine vinegar
- 1 teaspoon fresh thyme leaves
- salt and freshly ground black pepper

Directions:

1. Preheat the air fryer to 400°F.

2. Trim some of the fat from the duck. Rub olive oil on the duck and season with salt and pepper. Place the duck halves in the air fryer basket, breast side up and facing the center of the basket.

3. Air-fry the duck for 20 minutes. Turn the duck over and air-fry for another 6 minutes.

4. While duck is air-frying, make the cherry sauce. Melt the butter in a large sauté pan. Add the shallot and sauté until it is just starting to brown – about 2 to 3 minutes. Add the sherry and deglaze the pan by scraping up any brown bits from the bottom of the pan. Simmer the liquid for a few minutes, until it has reduced by half. Add the cherry preserves, chicken stock and white wine vinegar. Whisk well to combine all the ingredients. Simmer the sauce until it thickens and coats the back of a spoon – about 5 to 7 minutes. Season with salt and pepper and stir in the fresh thyme leaves.

5. When the air fryer timer goes off, spoon some cherry sauce over the duck and continue to air-fry at 400°F for 4 more minutes. Then, turn the duck halves back over so that the breast side is facing up. Spoon more cherry sauce over the top of the duck, covering the skin completely. Air-fry for 3 more minutes and then remove the duck to a plate to rest for a few minutes.

6. Serve the duck in halves, or cut each piece in half again for a smaller serving. Spoon any additional sauce over the duck or serve it on the side.

Chicken Strips

Servings: 4

Cooking Time: 8 Minutes

Ingredients:

- 1 pound chicken tenders
- Marinade
- ¼ cup olive oil
- 2 tablespoons water
- 2 tablespoons honey
- 2 tablespoons white vinegar
- ½ teaspoon salt
- ½ teaspoon crushed red pepper
- 1 teaspoon garlic powder
- 1 teaspoon onion powder
- ½ teaspoon paprika

Directions:

1. Combine all marinade ingredients and mix well.
2. Add chicken and stir to coat. Cover tightly and let marinate in refrigerator for 30minutes.
3. Remove tenders from marinade and place them in a single layer in the air fryer basket.
4. Cook at 390°F for 3minutes. Turn tenders over and cook for 5 minutes longer or until chicken is done and juices run clear.
5. Repeat step 4 to cook remaining tenders.

Buttermilk-fried Drumsticks

Servings: 2

Cooking Time: 25 Minutes

Ingredients:

- 1 egg
- ½ cup buttermilk
- ¾ cup self-rising flour
- ¾ cup seasoned panko breadcrumbs
- 1 teaspoon salt
- ¼ teaspoon ground black pepper (to mix into coating)
- 4 chicken drumsticks, skin on
- oil for misting or cooking spray

Directions:

1. Beat together egg and buttermilk in shallow dish.
2. In a second shallow dish, combine the flour, panko crumbs, salt, and pepper.
3. Sprinkle chicken legs with additional salt and pepper to taste.
4. Dip legs in buttermilk mixture, then roll in panko mixture, pressing in crumbs to make coating stick. Mist with oil or cooking spray.
5. Spray air fryer basket with cooking spray.
6. Cook drumsticks at 360°F for 10minutes. Turn pieces over and cook an additional 10minutes.
7. Turn pieces to check for browning. If you have any white spots that haven't begun to brown, spritz them with oil or cooking spray. Continue cooking for 5 more minutes or until crust is golden brown and juices run clear. Larger, meatier drumsticks will take longer to cook than small ones.

Southern-style Chicken Legs

Servings: 6

Cooking Time: 20 Minutes

Ingredients:

- 2 cups buttermilk
- 1 tablespoon hot sauce
- 12 chicken legs
- ½ teaspoon salt
- ½ teaspoon pepper
- 1 teaspoon paprika
- ½ teaspoon onion powder
- 1 teaspoon garlic powder
- 1 cup all-purpose flour

Directions:

1. In an airtight container, place the buttermilk, hot sauce, and chicken legs and refrigerate for 4 to 8 hours.

2. In a medium bowl, whisk together the salt, pepper, paprika, onion powder, garlic powder, and flour. Drain the chicken legs from the buttermilk and dip the chicken legs into the flour mixture, stirring to coat well.

3. Preheat the air fryer to 390°F.

4. Place the chicken legs in the air fryer basket and spray with cooking spray. Cook for 10 minutes, turn the chicken legs over, and cook for another 8 to 10 minutes. Check for an internal temperature of 165°F.

Gluten-free Nutty Chicken Fingers

Servings: 4

Cooking Time: 10 Minutes

Ingredients:

- ½ cup gluten-free flour
- ½ teaspoon garlic powder
- ¼ teaspoon onion powder
- ¼ teaspoon black pepper
- ¼ teaspoon salt
- 1 cup walnuts, pulsed into coarse flour
- ½ cup gluten-free breadcrumbs
- 2 large eggs
- 1 pound boneless, skinless chicken tenders

Directions:

1. Preheat the air fryer to 400°F.
2. In a medium bowl, mix the flour, garlic, onion, pepper, and salt. Set aside.
3. In a separate bowl, mix the walnut flour and breadcrumbs.
4. In a third bowl, whisk the eggs.
5. Liberally spray the air fryer basket with olive oil spray.
6. Pat the chicken tenders dry with a paper towel. Dredge the tenders one at a time in the flour, then dip them in the egg, and toss them in the breadcrumb coating. Repeat until all tenders are coated.
7. Set each tender in the air fryer, leaving room on each side of the tender to allow for flipping.
8. When the basket is full, cook 5 minutes, flip, and cook another 5 minutes. Check the internal temperature after cooking completes; it should read 165°F. If it does not, cook another 2 to 4 minutes.
9. Remove the tenders and let cool 5 minutes before serving. Repeat until all the tenders are cooked.

Teriyaki Chicken Drumsticks

Servings: 2

Cooking Time: 17 Minutes

Ingredients:

- 2 tablespoons soy sauce*
- ¼ cup dry sherry
- 1 tablespoon brown sugar
- 2 tablespoons water
- 1 tablespoon rice wine vinegar
- 1 clove garlic, crushed
- 1-inch fresh ginger, peeled and sliced
- pinch crushed red pepper flakes
- 4 to 6 bone-in, skin-on chicken drumsticks
- 1 tablespoon cornstarch
- fresh cilantro leaves

Directions:

1. Make the marinade by combining the soy sauce, dry sherry, brown sugar, water, rice vinegar, garlic, ginger and crushed red pepper flakes. Pour the marinade over the chicken legs, cover and let the chicken marinate for 1 to 4 hours in the refrigerator.

2. Preheat the air fryer to 380°F.

3. Transfer the chicken from the marinade to the air fryer basket, transferring any extra marinade to a small saucepan. Air-fry at 380°F for 8 minutes. Flip the chicken over and continue to air-fry for another 6 minutes, watching to make sure it doesn't brown too much.

4. While the chicken is cooking, bring the reserved marinade to a simmer on the stovetop. Dissolve the cornstarch in 2 tablespoons of water and stir this into the saucepan. Bring to a boil to thicken the sauce. Remove the garlic clove and slices of ginger from the sauce and set aside.

5. When the time is up on the air fryer, brush the thickened sauce on the chicken and air-fry for 3 more minutes. Remove the chicken from the air fryer and brush with the remaining sauce.

6. Serve over rice and sprinkle the cilantro leaves on top.

Simple Buttermilk Fried Chicken

Servings: 4   Cooking Time: 27 Minutes

Ingredients:

- 1 (4-pound) chicken, cut into 8 pieces
- 2 cups buttermilk
- hot sauce (optional)
- 1½ cups flour*
- 2 teaspoons paprika

- 1 teaspoon salt
- freshly ground black pepper
- 2 eggs, lightly beaten
- vegetable oil, in a spray bottle

Directions:

1. Cut the chicken into 8 pieces and submerge them in the buttermilk and hot sauce, if using. A zipper-sealable plastic bag works well for this. Let the chicken soak in the buttermilk for at least one hour or even overnight in the refrigerator.

2. Set up a dredging station. Mix the flour, paprika, salt and black pepper in a clean zipper-sealable plastic bag. Whisk the eggs and place them in a shallow dish. Remove four pieces of chicken from the buttermilk and transfer them to the bag with the flour. Shake them around to coat on all sides. Remove the chicken from the flour, shaking off any excess flour, and dip them into the beaten egg. Return the chicken to the bag of seasoned flour and shake again. Set the coated chicken aside and repeat with the remaining four pieces of chicken.

3. Preheat the air fryer to 370°F.

4. Spray the chicken on all sides with the vegetable oil and then transfer one batch to the air fryer basket. Air-fry the chicken at 370°F for 20 minutes, flipping the pieces over halfway through the cooking process, taking care not to knock off the breading. Transfer the chicken to a plate, but do not cover. Repeat with the second batch of chicken.

5. Lower the temperature on the air fryer to 340°F. Flip the chicken back over and place the first batch of chicken on top of the second batch already in the basket. Air-fry for another 7 minutes and serve warm.

Coconut Chicken With Apricot-ginger Sauce

Servings: 4   Cooking Time: 8 Minutes Per Batch

Ingredients:

- 1½ pounds boneless, skinless chicken tenders, cut in large chunks (about 1¼ inches)
- salt and pepper
- ½ cup cornstarch
- 2 eggs
- 1 tablespoon milk
- 3 cups shredded coconut (see below)
- oil for misting or cooking spray
- Apricot-Ginger Sauce
- ½ cup apricot preserves
- 2 tablespoons white vinegar
- ¼ teaspoon ground ginger
- ¼ teaspoon low-sodium soy sauce
- 2 teaspoons white or yellow onion, grated or finely minced

Directions:

1. Mix all ingredients for the Apricot-Ginger Sauce well and let sit for flavors to blend while you cook the chicken.
2. Season chicken chunks with salt and pepper to taste.
3. Place cornstarch in a shallow dish.
4. In another shallow dish, beat together eggs and milk.
5. Place coconut in a third shallow dish. (If also using panko breadcrumbs, as suggested below, stir them to mix well.)
6. Spray air fryer basket with oil or cooking spray.
7. Dip each chicken chunk into cornstarch, shake off excess, and dip in egg mixture.
8. Shake off excess egg mixture and roll lightly in coconut or coconut mixture. Spray with oil.
9. Place coated chicken chunks in air fryer basket in a single layer, close together but without sides touching.
10. Cook at 360°F for 4minutes, stop, and turn chunks over.
11. Cook an additional 4 minutes or until chicken is done inside and coating is crispy brown.
12. Repeat steps 9 through 11 to cook remaining chicken chunks.

Apricot Glazed Chicken Thighs

Servings: 2

Cooking Time: 22 Minutes

Ingredients:

- 4 bone-in chicken thighs (about 2 pounds)
- olive oil
- 1 teaspoon salt
- ¼ teaspoon freshly ground black pepper
- ½ teaspoon onion powder
- ¾ cup apricot preserves 1½ tablespoons Dijon mustard
- ½ teaspoon dried thyme
- 1 teaspoon soy sauce
- fresh thyme leaves, for garnish

Directions:

1. Preheat the air fryer to 380°F.

2. Brush or spray both the air fryer basket and the chicken with the olive oil. Combine the salt, pepper and onion powder and season both sides of the chicken with the spice mixture.

3. Place the seasoned chicken thighs, skin side down in the air fryer basket. Air-fry for 10 minutes.

4. While chicken is cooking, make the glaze by combining the apricot preserves, Dijon mustard, thyme and soy sauce in a small bowl.

5. When the time is up on the air fryer, spoon half of the apricot glaze over the chicken thighs and air-fry for 2 minutes. Then flip the chicken thighs over so that the skin side is facing up and air-fry for an additional 8 minutes. Finally, spoon and spread the rest of the glaze evenly over the chicken thighs and air-fry for a final 2 minutes. Transfer the chicken to a serving platter and sprinkle the fresh thyme leaves on top.

Appetizers And Snacks

Fried Green Tomatoes

Servings: 4   Cooking Time: 15 Minutes

Ingredients:

- 2 eggs
- ¼ cup buttermilk
- ½ cup cornmeal
- ½ cup breadcrumbs
- ¼ teaspoon salt
- 1½ pounds firm green tomatoes, cut in ¼-inch slices
- oil for misting or cooking spray

- Horseradish Drizzle
- ¼ cup mayonnaise
- ¼ cup sour cream
- 2 teaspoons prepared horseradish
- ½ teaspoon Worcestershire sauce
- ½ teaspoon lemon juice
- ⅛ teaspoon black pepper

Directions:

1. Mix all ingredients for Horseradish Drizzle together and chill while you prepare the green tomatoes.
2. Preheat air fryer to 390°F.
3. Beat the eggs and buttermilk together in a shallow bowl.
4. Mix cornmeal, breadcrumbs, and salt together in a plate or shallow dish.
5. Dip 4 tomato slices in the egg mixture, then roll in the breadcrumb mixture.
6. Mist one side with oil and place in air fryer basket, oil-side down, in a single layer.
7. Mist the top with oil.
8. Cook for 15minutes, turning once, until brown and crispy.
9. Repeat steps 5 through 8 to cook remaining tomatoes.
10. Drizzle horseradish sauce over tomatoes just before serving.

Indian Cauliflower Tikka Bites

Servings: 6

Cooking Time: 20 Minutes

Ingredients:

- 1 cup plain Greek yogurt
- 1 teaspoon fresh ginger
- 1 teaspoon minced garlic
- 1 teaspoon vindaloo
- ½ teaspoon cardamom
- ½ teaspoon paprika
- ½ teaspoon turmeric powder
- ½ teaspoon cumin powder
- 1 large head of cauliflower, washed and cut into medium-size florets
- ½ cup panko breadcrumbs
- 1 lemon, quartered

Directions:

1. Preheat the air fryer to 350°F.

2. In a large bowl, mix the yogurt, ginger, garlic, vindaloo, cardamom, paprika, turmeric, and cumin. Add the cauliflower florets to the bowl, and coat them with the yogurt.

3. Remove the cauliflower florets from the bowl and place them on a baking sheet. Sprinkle the panko breadcrumbs over the top. Place the cauliflower bites into the air fryer basket, leaving space between the florets. Depending on the size of your air fryer, you may need to make more than one batch.

4. Cook the cauliflower for 10 minutes, shake the basket, and continue cooking another 10 minutes (or until the florets are lightly browned).

5. Remove from the air fryer and keep warm. Continue to cook until all the florets are done.

6. Before serving, lightly squeeze lemon over the top. Serve warm.

Spicy Sweet Potato Tater-tots

Servings: 6

Cooking Time: 10 Minutes

Ingredients:

- 6 cups filtered water
- 2 medium sweet potatoes, peeled and cut in half
- 1 teaspoon garlic powder
- ½ teaspoon black pepper, divided
- ½ teaspoon salt, divided
- 1 cup panko breadcrumbs
- 1 teaspoon blackened seasoning

Directions:

1. In a large stovetop pot, bring the water to a boil. Add the sweet potatoes and let boil about 10 minutes, until a metal fork prong can be inserted but the potatoes still have a slight give (not completely mashed).

2. Carefully remove the potatoes from the pot and let cool.

3. When you're able to touch them, grate the potatoes into a large bowl. Mix the garlic powder, ¼ teaspoon of the black pepper, and ¼ teaspoon of the salt into the potatoes. Place the mixture in the refrigerator and let set at least 45 minutes (if you're leaving them longer than 45 minutes, cover the bowl).

4. Before assembling, mix the breadcrumbs and blackened seasoning in a small bowl.

5. Remove the sweet potatoes from the refrigerator and preheat the air fryer to 400°F.

6. Assemble the tater-tots by using a teaspoon to portion batter evenly and form into a tater-tot shape. Roll each tater-tot in the breadcrumb mixture. Then carefully place the tater-tots in the air fryer basket. Be sure that you've liberally sprayed the air fryer basket with an olive oil mist. Repeat until tater-tots fill the basket without touching one another. You'll need to do multiple batches, depending on the size of your air fryer.

7. Cook the tater-tots for 3 to 6 minutes, flip, and cook another 3 to 6 minutes.

8. Remove from the air fryer carefully and keep warm until ready to serve.

Polenta Fries With Chili-lime Mayo

Servings: 4

Cooking Time: 28 Minutes

Ingredients:

- 2 teaspoons vegetable or olive oil
- ¼ teaspoon paprika
- 1 pound prepared polenta, cut into 3-inch x ½-inch sticks
- salt and freshly ground black pepper
- Chili-Lime Mayo
- ½ cup mayonnaise
- 1 teaspoon chili powder
- ¼ teaspoon ground cumin
- juice of half a lime
- 1 teaspoon chopped fresh cilantro
- salt and freshly ground black pepper

Directions:

1. Preheat the air fryer to 400°F.
2. Combine the oil and paprika and then carefully toss the polenta sticks in the mixture.
3. Air-fry the polenta fries at 400°F for 15 minutes. Gently shake the basket to rotate the fries and continue to air-fry for another 13 minutes or until the fries have browned nicely. Season to taste with salt and freshly ground black pepper.
4. To make the chili-lime mayo, combine all the ingredients in a small bowl and stir well.
5. Serve the polenta fries warm with chili-lime mayo on the side for dipping.

Smoked Salmon Puffs

Servings: 2

Cooking Time: 8 Minutes

Ingredients:

- Two quarters of one thawed sheet (that is, a half of the sheet; wrap and refreeze the remainder) A 17.25-ounce box frozen puff pastry
- 4 ½-ounce smoked salmon slices
- 2 tablespoons Softened regular or low-fat cream cheese (not fat-free)
- Up to 2 teaspoons Drained and rinsed capers, minced
- Up to 2 teaspoons Minced red onion
- 1 Large egg white
- 1 tablespoon Water

Directions:

1. Preheat the air fryer to 400°F.
2. For a small air fryer, roll the piece of puff pastry into a 6 x 6-inch square on a clean, dry work surface.
3. For a medium or larger air fryer, roll each piece of puff pastry into a 6 x 6-inch square.
4. Set 2 salmon slices on the diagonal, corner to corner, on each rolled-out sheet. Smear the salmon with cream cheese, then sprinkle with capers and red onion. Fold the sheet closed by picking up one corner that does not have an edge of salmon near it and folding the dough across the salmon to its opposite corner. Seal the edges closed by pressing the tines of a flatware fork into them.
5. Whisk the egg white and water in a small bowl until uniform. Brush this mixture over the top(s) of the packet(s).
6. Set the packet(s) in the basket (if you're working with more than one, they cannot touch). Air-fry undisturbed for 8 minutes, or until golden brown and flaky.
7. Use a nonstick-safe spatula to transfer the packet(s) to a wire rack. Cool for 5 minutes before serving.

Fried Cheese Ravioli With Marinara Sauce

Servings: 4

Cooking Time: 7 Minutes

Ingredients:

- 1 pound cheese ravioli, fresh or frozen
- 2 eggs, lightly beaten
- 1 cup plain breadcrumbs
- ½ teaspoon paprika
- ½ teaspoon dried oregano
- ½ teaspoon salt
- grated Parmesan cheese
- chopped fresh parsley
- 1 to 2 cups marinara sauce (jarred or homemade)

Directions:

1. Bring a stockpot of salted water to a boil. Boil the ravioli according to the package directions and then drain. Let the cooked ravioli cool to a temperature where you can comfortably handle them.

2. While the pasta is cooking, set up a dredging station with two shallow dishes. Place the eggs into one dish. Combine the breadcrumbs, paprika, dried oregano and salt in the other dish.

3. Preheat the air fryer to 380°F.

4. Working with one at a time, dip the cooked ravioli into the egg, coating all sides. Then press the ravioli into the breadcrumbs, making sure that all sides are covered. Transfer the ravioli to the air fryer basket, cooking in batches, one layer at a time. Air-fry at 380°F for 7 minutes.

5. While the ravioli is air-frying, bring the marinara sauce to a simmer on the stovetop. Transfer to a small bowl.

6. Sprinkle a little Parmesan cheese and chopped parsley on top of the fried ravioli and serve warm with the marinara sauce on the side for dipping.

String Bean Fries

Servings: 4

Cooking Time: 6 Minutes

Ingredients:

- ½ pound fresh string beans
- 2 eggs
- 4 teaspoons water
- ½ cup white flour
- ½ cup breadcrumbs
- ¼ teaspoon salt
- ¼ teaspoon ground black pepper
- ¼ teaspoon dry mustard (optional)
- oil for misting or cooking spray

Directions:

1. Preheat air fryer to 360°F.
2. Trim stem ends from string beans, wash, and pat dry.
3. In a shallow dish, beat eggs and water together until well blended.
4. Place flour in a second shallow dish.
5. In a third shallow dish, stir together the breadcrumbs, salt, pepper, and dry mustard if using.
6. Dip each string bean in egg mixture, flour, egg mixture again, then breadcrumbs.
7. When you finish coating all the string beans, open air fryer and place them in basket.
8. Cook for 3minutes.
9. Stop and mist string beans with oil or cooking spray.
10. Cook for 3 moreminutes or until string beans are crispy and nicely browned.

Garlic Wings

Servings: 4

Cooking Time: 15 Minutes

Ingredients:

- 2 pounds chicken wings
- oil for misting
- cooking spray
- Marinade
- 1 cup buttermilk
- 2 cloves garlic, mashed flat
- 1 teaspoon Worcestershire sauce
- 1 bay leaf
- Coating
- 1½ cups grated Parmesan cheese
- ¾ cup breadcrumbs
- 1½ tablespoons garlic powder
- ½ teaspoon salt

Directions:

1. Mix all marinade ingredients together.

2. Remove wing tips (the third joint) and discard or freeze for stock. Cut the remaining wings at the joint and toss them into the marinade, stirring to coat well. Refrigerate for at least an hour but no more than 8 hours.

3. When ready to cook, combine all coating ingredients in a shallow dish.

4. Remove wings from marinade, shaking off excess, and roll in coating mixture. Press coating into wings so that it sticks well. Spray wings with oil.

5. Spray air fryer basket with cooking spray. Place wings in basket in single layer, close but not touching.

6. Cook at 360°F for 15minutes or until chicken is done and juices run clear.

7. Repeat previous step to cook remaining wings.

Spanakopita Spinach, Feta And Pine Nut Phyllo Bites

Servings: 8   Cooking Time: 10 Minutes

Ingredients:

- ½ (10-ounce) package frozen spinach, thawed and squeezed dry (about 1 cup)
- ¾ cup crumbled feta cheese
- ¼ cup grated Parmesan cheese
- ¼ cup pine nuts, toasted
- ⅛ teaspoon ground nutmeg
- 1 egg, lightly beaten
- ½ teaspoon salt
- freshly ground black pepper
- 6 sheets phyllo dough
- ½ cup butter, melted

Directions:

1. Combine the spinach, cheeses, pine nuts, nutmeg and egg in a bowl. Season with salt and freshly ground black pepper.

2. While building the phyllo triangles, always keep the dough sheets you are not working with covered with plastic wrap and a damp clean kitchen towel. Remove one sheet of the phyllo and place it on a flat surface. Brush the phyllo sheet with melted butter and then layer another sheet of phyllo on top. Brush the second sheet of phyllo with butter. Cut the layered phyllo sheets into 6 strips, about 2½- to 3-inches wide.

3. Place a heaping tablespoon of the spinach filling at the end of each strip of dough. Fold the bottom right corner of the strip over the filling towards the left edge of the strip to make a triangle. Continue to fold the phyllo dough around the spinach as you would fold a flag, making triangle after triangle. Brush the outside of the phyllo triangle with more melted butter and set it aside until you've finished the 6 strips of dough, making 6 triangles.

4. Preheat the air fryer to 350°F.

5. Transfer the first six phyllo triangles to the air fryer basket and air-fry for 5 minutes. Turn the triangles over and air-fry for another 5 minutes.

6. While the first batch of triangles is air-frying, build another set of triangles and air-fry in the same manner. You should do three batches total. These can be warmed in the air fryer for a minute or two just before serving if you like.

Crispy Tofu Bites

Servings: 4

Cooking Time: 20 Minutes

Ingredients:

- 1 pound Extra firm unflavored tofu
- Vegetable oil spray

Directions:

1. Wrap the piece of tofu in a triple layer of paper towels. Place it on a wooden cutting board and set a large pot on top of it to press out excess moisture. Set aside for 10 minutes.

2. Preheat the air fryer to 400°F.

3. Remove the pot and unwrap the tofu. Cut it into 1-inch cubes. Place these in a bowl and coat them generously with vegetable oil spray. Toss gently, then spray generously again before tossing, until all are glistening.

4. Gently pour the tofu pieces into the basket, spread them into as close to one layer as possible, and air-fry for 20 minutes, using kitchen tongs to gently rearrange the pieces at the 7- and 14-minute marks, until light brown and crisp.

5. Gently pour the tofu pieces onto a wire rack. Cool for 5 minutes before serving warm.

Homemade French Fries

Servings: 2

Cooking Time: 25 Minutes

Ingredients:

- 2 to 3 russet potatoes, peeled and cut into ½-inch sticks
- 2 to 3 teaspoons olive or vegetable oil
- salt

Directions:

1. Bring a large saucepan of salted water to a boil on the stovetop while you peel and cut the potatoes. Blanch the potatoes in the boiling salted water for 4 minutes while you Preheat the air fryer to 400°F. Strain the potatoes and rinse them with cold water. Dry them well with a clean kitchen towel.

2. Toss the dried potato sticks gently with the oil and place them in the air fryer basket. Air-fry for 25 minutes, shaking the basket a few times while the fries cook to help them brown evenly. Season the fries with salt mid-way through cooking and serve them warm with tomato ketchup, Sriracha mayonnaise or a mix of lemon zest, Parmesan cheese and parsley.

Stuffed Mushrooms

Servings: 10

Cooking Time: 8 Minutes

Ingredients:

- 8 ounces white mushroom caps, stems removed
- salt
- 6 fresh mozzarella cheese balls
- ground dried thyme
- ¼ roasted red pepper cut into small pieces (about ½ inch)

Directions:

1. Sprinkle inside of mushroom caps with salt to taste.
2. Cut mozzarella balls in half.
3. Stuff each cap with half a mozzarella cheese ball. Sprinkle very lightly with thyme.
4. Top each mushroom with a small strip of roasted red pepper, lightly pressing it into the cheese.
5. Cook at 390°F for 8minutes or longer if you prefer softer mushrooms.

Vegetable Side Dishes Recipes

Florentine Stuffed Tomatoes

Servings: 2

Cooking Time: 12 Minutes

Ingredients:

- 1 cup frozen spinach, thawed and squeezed dry
- ¼ cup toasted pine nuts
- ¼ cup grated mozzarella cheese
- ½ cup crumbled feta cheese
- ½ cup coarse fresh breadcrumbs
- 1 tablespoon olive oil
- salt and freshly ground black pepper
- 2 to 3 beefsteak tomatoes, halved horizontally and insides scooped out

Directions:

1. Combine the spinach, pine nuts, mozzarella and feta cheeses, breadcrumbs, olive oil, salt and freshly ground black pepper in a bowl. Spoon the mixture into the tomato halves. You should have enough filling for 2 to 3 tomatoes, depending on how big they are.

2. Preheat the air fryer to 350°F.

3. Place three or four tomato halves (depending on whether you're using 2 or 3 tomatoes and how big they are) into the air fryer and air-fry for 12 minutes. The tomatoes should be soft but still manageable and the tops should be lightly browned. Repeat with second batch if necessary.

4. Let the tomatoes cool for just a minute or two before serving.

Parmesan Garlic Fries

Servings: 4

Cooking Time: 20 Minutes

Ingredients:

- 2 medium Yukon gold potatoes, washed
- 1 tablespoon extra-virgin olive oil
- 1 garlic clove, minced
- 2 tablespoons finely grated parmesan cheese
- ¼ teaspoon black pepper
- ¼ teaspoon salt
- 1 tablespoon freshly chopped parsley

Directions:

1. Preheat the air fryer to 400°F.

2. Slice the potatoes into long strips about ¼-inch thick. In a large bowl, toss the potatoes with the olive oil, garlic, cheese, pepper, and salt.

3. Place the fries into the air fryer basket and cook for 4 minutes; shake the basket and cook another 4 minutes.

4. Remove and serve warm.

Fried Green Tomatoes With Sriracha Mayo

Servings: 4   Cooking Time: 12 Minutes

Ingredients:

- 3 green tomatoes
- salt and freshly ground black pepper
- ⅓ cup all-purpose flour*
- 2 eggs
- ½ cup buttermilk
- 1 cup panko breadcrumbs*
- 1 cup cornmeal
- olive oil, in a spray bottle
- fresh thyme sprigs or chopped fresh chives
- Sriracha Mayo
- ½ cup mayonnaise
- 1 to 2 tablespoons sriracha hot sauce
- 1 tablespoon milk

Directions:

1. Cut the tomatoes in ¼-inch slices. Pat them dry with a clean kitchen towel and season generously with salt and pepper.

2. Set up a dredging station using three shallow dishes. Place the flour in the first shallow dish, whisk the eggs and buttermilk together in the second dish, and combine the panko breadcrumbs and cornmeal in the third dish.

3. Preheat the air fryer to 400°F.

4. Dredge the tomato slices in flour to coat on all sides. Then dip them into the egg mixture and finally press them into the breadcrumbs to coat all sides of the tomato.

5. Spray or brush the air-fryer basket with olive oil. Transfer 3 to 4 tomato slices into the basket and spray the top with olive oil. Air-fry the tomatoes at 400°F for 8 minutes. Flip them over, spray the other side with oil and air-fry for an additional 4 minutes until golden brown.

6. While the tomatoes are cooking, make the sriracha mayo. Combine the mayonnaise, 1 tablespoon of the sriracha hot sauce and milk in a small bowl. Stir well until the mixture is smooth. Add more sriracha sauce to taste.

7. When the tomatoes are done, transfer them to a cooling rack or a platter lined with paper towels so the bottom does not get soggy. Before serving, carefully stack the all the tomatoes into air fryer and air-fry at 350°F for 1 to 2 minutes to heat them back up.

8. Serve the fried green tomatoes hot with the sriracha mayo on the side. Season one last time with salt and freshly ground black pepper and garnish with sprigs of fresh thyme or chopped fresh chives.

Honey-roasted Parsnips

Servings: 3

Cooking Time: 23 Minutes

Ingredients:

- 1½ pounds Medium parsnips, peeled
- Olive oil spray
- 1 tablespoon Honey
- 1½ teaspoons Water
- ¼ teaspoon Table salt

Directions:

1. Preheat the air fryer to 350°F .

2. If the thick end of a parsnip is more than ½ inch in diameter, cut the parsnip just below where it swells to its large end, then slice the large section in half lengthwise. If the parsnips are larger than the basket (or basket attachment), trim off the thin end so the parsnips will fit. Generously coat the parsnips on all sides with olive oil spray.

3. When the machine is at temperature, set the parsnips in the basket with as much air space between them as possible. Air-fry undisturbed for 20 minutes.

4. Whisk the honey, water, and salt in a small bowl until smooth. Brush this mixture over the parsnips. Air-fry undisturbed for 3 minutes more, or until the glaze is lightly browned.

5. Use kitchen tongs to transfer the parsnips to a wire rack or a serving platter. Cool for a couple of minutes before serving.

Hush Puppies

Servings: 8

Cooking Time: 11 Minutes

Ingredients:

- ½ cup Whole or low-fat milk (not fat-free)
- 1½ tablespoons Butter
- ½ cup plus 1 tablespoon, plus more All-purpose flour
- ½ cup plus 1 tablespoon Yellow cornmeal
- 2 teaspoons Granulated white sugar
- 2 teaspoons Baking powder
- ¾ teaspoon Baking soda
- ¾ teaspoon Table salt
- ¼ teaspoon Onion powder
- 3 tablespoons (or 1 medium egg, well beaten) Pasteurized egg substitute, such as Egg Beaters
- Vegetable oil spray

Directions:

1. Heat the milk and butter in a small saucepan set over medium heat just until the butter melts and the milk is steamy. Do not simmer or boil.

2. Meanwhile, whisk the flour, cornmeal, sugar, baking powder, baking soda, salt, and onion powder in a large bowl until the mixture is a uniform color.

3. Stir the hot milk mixture into the flour mixture to form a dough. Set aside to cool for 5 minutes.

4. Mix the egg substitute or egg into the dough to make a thick, smooth batter. Cover and refrigerate for at least 1 hour or up to 4 hours.

5. Preheat the air fryer to 350°F .

6. Lightly flour your clean, dry hands. Roll 2 tablespoons of the batter into a ball between your floured palms. Set aside, flour your hands again if necessary, and continue making more balls with the remaining batter.

7. Coat the balls all over with the vegetable oil spray. Line the machine's basket (or basket attachment) with a piece of parchment paper. Set the balls on the parchment paper with as much air space between them as possible. Air-fry for 9 minutes, or until lightly browned and set.

8. Use kitchen tongs to gently transfer the hush puppies to a wire rack. Cool for at least 5 minutes before serving. Or cool to room temperature, about 45 minutes, and store in a sealed container at room temperature for up to 2 days. To crisp the hush puppies again, put them in a 350°F air fryer for 2 minutes. (There's no need for parchment paper in the machine during reheating.)

Creole Potato Wedges

Servings: 4

Cooking Time: 10 Minutes

Ingredients:

- 1 pound medium Yukon gold potatoes
- ½ teaspoon cayenne pepper
- ½ teaspoon thyme
- ½ teaspoon garlic powder
- ½ teaspoon salt
- ½ teaspoon smoked paprika
- 1 cup dry breadcrumbs
- oil for misting or cooking spray

Directions:

1. Wash potatoes, cut into thick wedges, and drop wedges into a bowl of water to prevent browning.

2. Mix together the cayenne pepper, thyme, garlic powder, salt, paprika, and breadcrumbs and spread on a sheet of wax paper.

3. Remove potatoes from water and, without drying them, roll in the breadcrumb mixture.

4. Spray air fryer basket with oil or cooking spray and pile potato wedges into basket. It's okay if they form more than a single layer.

5. Cook at 390°F for 8minutes. Shake basket, then continue cooking for 2 minutes longer, until coating is crisp and potato centers are soft. Total cooking time will vary, depending on thickness of potato wedges.

Panko-crusted Zucchini Fries

Servings: 6

Cooking Time: 8 Minutes

Ingredients:

- 3 medium zucchinis
- ½ cup flour
- 1 teaspoon salt, divided
- ½ teaspoon black pepper, divided
- ¾ teaspoon dried thyme, divided
- 2 large eggs
- 1 ½ cups whole-wheat or plain panko breadcrumbs
- ½ cup grated Parmesan cheese

Directions:

1. Preheat the air fryer to 380°F.

2. Slice the zucchinis in half lengthwise, then into long strips about ½-inch thick, like thick fries.

3. In a medium bowl, mix the flour, ½ teaspoon of the salt, ¼ teaspoon of the black pepper, and ½ teaspoon of thyme.

4. In a separate bowl, whisk together the eggs, ½ teaspoon of the salt, and ¼ teaspoon of the black pepper.

5. In a third bowl, combine the breadcrumbs, cheese, and the remaining ¼ teaspoon of dried thyme.

6. Working with one zucchini fry at a time, dip the zucchini fry first into the flour mixture, then into the whisked eggs, and finally into the breading. Repeat until all the fries are breaded.

7. Place the zucchini fries into the air fryer basket, spray with cooking spray, and cook for 4 minutes; shake the basket and cook another 4 to 6 minutes or until golden brown and crispy.

8. Remove and serve warm.

Mushrooms

Servings: 4

Cooking Time: 12 Minutes

Ingredients:

- 8 ounces whole white button mushrooms
- ½ teaspoon salt
- ⅛ teaspoon pepper
- ¼ teaspoon garlic powder
- ¼ teaspoon onion powder
- 5 tablespoons potato starch
- 1 egg, beaten
- ¾ cup panko breadcrumbs
- oil for misting or cooking spray

Directions:

1. Place mushrooms in a large bowl. Add the salt, pepper, garlic and onion powders, and stir well to distribute seasonings.

2. Add potato starch to mushrooms and toss in bowl until well coated.

3. Dip mushrooms in beaten egg, roll in panko crumbs, and mist with oil or cooking spray.

4. Place mushrooms in air fryer basket. You can cook them all at once, and it's okay if a few are stacked.

5. Cook at 390°F for 5minutes. Shake basket, then continue cooking for 7 more minutes, until golden brown and crispy.

Salmon Salad With Steamboat Dressing

Servings: 4

Cooking Time: 18 Minutes

Ingredients:

- ¼ teaspoon salt
- 1½ teaspoons dried dill weed
- 1 tablespoon fresh lemon juice
- 8 ounces fresh or frozen salmon fillet (skin on)
- 8 cups shredded romaine, Boston, or other leaf lettuce
- 8 spears cooked asparagus, cut in 1-inch pieces
- 8 cherry tomatoes, halved or quartered

Directions:

1. Mix the salt and dill weed together. Rub the lemon juice over the salmon on both sides and sprinkle the dill and salt all over. Refrigerate for 15 to 20minutes.

2. Make Steamboat Dressing and refrigerate while cooking salmon and preparing salad.

3. Cook salmon in air fryer basket at 330°F for 18 minutes. Cooking time will vary depending on thickness of fillets. When done, salmon should flake with fork but still be moist and tender.

4. Remove salmon from air fryer and cool slightly. At this point, the skin should slide off easily. Cut salmon into 4 pieces and discard skin.

5. Divide the lettuce among 4 plates. Scatter asparagus spears and tomato pieces evenly over the lettuce, allowing roughly 2 whole spears and 2 whole cherry tomatoes per plate.

6. Top each salad with one portion of the salmon and drizzle with a tablespoon of dressing. Serve with additional dressing to pass at the table.

Roasted Ratatouille Vegetables

Servings: 2

Cooking Time: 15 Minutes

Ingredients:

- 1 baby or Japanese eggplant, cut into 1½-inch cubes
- 1 red pepper, cut into 1-inch chunks
- 1 yellow pepper, cut into 1-inch chunks
- 1 zucchini, cut into 1-inch chunks
- 1 clove garlic, minced
- ½ teaspoon dried basil
- 1 tablespoon olive oil
- salt and freshly ground black pepper
- ¼ cup sliced sun-dried tomatoes in oil
- 2 tablespoons chopped fresh basil

Directions:

1. Preheat the air fryer to 400°F.

2. Toss the eggplant, peppers and zucchini with the garlic, dried basil, olive oil, salt and freshly ground black pepper.

3. Air-fry the vegetables at 400°F for 15 minutes, shaking the basket a few times during the cooking process to redistribute the ingredients.

4. As soon as the vegetables are tender, toss them with the sliced sun-dried tomatoes and fresh basil and serve.

Perfect French Fries

Servings: 3

Cooking Time: 37 Minutes

Ingredients:

- 1 pound Large russet potato(es)
- Vegetable oil or olive oil spray
- ½ teaspoon Table salt

Directions:

1. Cut each potato lengthwise into ¼-inch-thick slices. Cut each of these lengthwise into ¼-inch-thick matchsticks.

2. Set the potato matchsticks in a big bowl of cool water and soak for 5 minutes. Drain in a colander set in the sink, then spread the matchsticks out on paper towels and dry them very well.

3. Preheat the air fryer to 225°F (or 230°F, if that's the closest setting).

4. When the machine is at temperature, arrange the matchsticks in an even layer (if overlapping but not compact) in the basket. Air-fry for 20 minutes, tossing and rearranging the fries twice.

5. Pour the contents of the basket into a big bowl. Increase the air fryer's temperature to 325°F (or 330°F, if that's the closest setting).

6. Generously coat the fries with vegetable or olive oil spray. Toss well, then coat them again to make sure they're covered on all sides, tossing (and maybe spraying) a couple of times to make sure.

7. When the machine is at temperature, pour the fries into the basket and air-fry for 12 minutes, tossing and rearranging the fries at least twice.

8. Increase the machine's temperature to 375°F (or 380°F or 390°F, if one of these is the closest setting). Air-fry for 5 minutes more (from the moment you raise the temperature), tossing and rearranging the fries at least twice to keep them from burning and to make sure they all get an even measure of the heat, until brown and crisp.

9. Pour the contents of the basket into a serving bowl. Toss the fries with the salt and serve hot.

Fingerling Potatoes

Servings: 4

Cooking Time: 15 Minutes

Ingredients:

- 1 pound fingerling potatoes
- 1 tablespoon light olive oil
- ½ teaspoon dried parsley
- ½ teaspoon lemon juice
- coarsely ground sea salt

Directions:

1. Cut potatoes in half lengthwise.

2. In a large bowl, combine potatoes, oil, parsley, and lemon juice. Stir well to coat potatoes.

3. Place potatoes in air fryer basket and cook at 360°F for 15 minutes or until lightly browned and tender inside.

4. Sprinkle with sea salt before serving.

Beef，Pork & Lamb Recipes

Pork Schnitzel With Dill Sauce

Servings: 4   Cooking Time: 4 Minutes

Ingredients:

- 6 boneless, center cut pork chops (about 1½ pounds)
- ½ cup flour
- 1½ teaspoons salt
- freshly ground black pepper
- 2 eggs
- ½ cup milk
- 1½ cups toasted fine breadcrumbs
- 1 teaspoon paprika
- 3 tablespoons butter, melted
- 2 tablespoons vegetable or olive oil
- lemon wedges
- Dill Sauce:
- 1 cup chicken stock
- 1½ tablespoons cornstarch
- ⅓ cup sour cream
- 1½ tablespoons chopped fresh dill
- salt and pepper

Directions:

1. Trim the excess fat from the pork chops and pound each chop with a meat mallet between two pieces of plastic wrap until they are ½-inch thick.

2. Set up a dredging station. Combine the flour, salt, and black pepper in a shallow dish. Whisk the eggs and milk together in a second shallow dish. Finally, combine the breadcrumbs and paprika in a third shallow dish.

3. Dip each flattened pork chop in the flour. Shake off the excess flour and dip each chop into the egg mixture. Finally dip them into the breadcrumbs and press the breadcrumbs onto the meat firmly. Place each finished chop on a baking sheet until they are all coated.

4. Preheat the air fryer to 400°F.

5. Combine the melted butter and the oil in a small bowl and lightly brush both sides of the coated pork chops. Do not brush the chops too heavily or the breading will not be as crispy.

6. Air-fry one schnitzel at a time for 4 minutes, turning it over halfway through the cooking time. Hold the cooked schnitzels warm on a baking pan in a 170°F oven while you finish air-frying the rest.

7. While the schnitzels are cooking, whisk the chicken stock and cornstarch together in a small saucepan over medium-high heat on the stovetop. Bring the mixture to a boil and simmer for 2 minutes.

Remove the saucepan from heat and whisk in the sour cream. Add the chopped fresh dill and season with salt and pepper.

8. Transfer the pork schnitzel to a platter and serve with dill sauce and lemon wedges. For a traditional meal, serve this along side some egg noodles, spätzle or German potato salad.

Crispy Pierogi With Kielbasa And Onions

Servings: 3

Cooking Time: 20 Minutes

Ingredients:

- 6 Frozen potato and cheese pierogi, thawed (about 12 pierogi to 1 pound)
- ½ pound Smoked kielbasa, sliced into ½-inch-thick rounds
- ¾ cup Very roughly chopped sweet onion, preferably Vidalia
- Vegetable oil spray

Directions:

1. Preheat the air fryer to 375°F .

2. Put the pierogi, kielbasa rounds, and onion in a large bowl. Coat them with vegetable oil spray, toss well, spray again, and toss until everything is glistening.

3. When the machine is at temperature, dump the contents of the bowl it into the basket. (Items may be leaning against each other and even on top of each other.) Air-fry, tossing and rearranging everything twice so that all covered surfaces get exposed, for 20 minutes, or until the sausages have begun to brown and the pierogi are crisp.

4. Pour the contents of the basket onto a serving platter. Wait a minute or two just to take make sure nothing's searing hot before serving.

Indian Fry Bread Tacos

Servings: 4

Cooking Time: 20 Minutes

Ingredients:

- 1 cup all-purpose flour
- 1½ teaspoons salt, divided
- 1½ teaspoons baking powder
- ¼ cup milk
- ¼ cup warm water
- ½ pound lean ground beef
- One 14.5-ounce can pinto beans, drained and rinsed
- 1 tablespoon taco seasoning
- ½ cup shredded cheddar cheese
- 2 cups shredded lettuce
- ¼ cup black olives, chopped
- 1 Roma tomato, diced
- 1 avocado, diced
- 1 lime

Directions:

1. In a large bowl, whisk together the flour, 1 teaspoon of the salt, and baking powder. Make a well in the center and add in the milk and water. Form a ball and gently knead the dough four times. Cover the bowl with a damp towel, and set aside.

2. Preheat the air fryer to 380°F.

3. In a medium bowl, mix together the ground beef, beans, and taco seasoning. Crumble the meat mixture into the air fryer basket and cook for 5 minutes; toss the meat and cook an additional 2 to 3 minutes, or until cooked fully. Place the cooked meat in a bowl for taco assembly; season with the remaining ½ teaspoon salt as desired.

4. On a floured surface, place the dough. Cut the dough into 4 equal parts. Using a rolling pin, roll out each piece of dough to 5 inches in diameter. Spray the dough with cooking spray and place in the air fryer basket, working in batches as needed. Cook for 3 minutes, flip over, spray with cooking spray, and cook for an additional 1 to 3 minutes, until golden and puffy.

5. To assemble, place the fry breads on a serving platter. Equally divide the meat and bean mixture on top of the fry bread. Divide the cheese, lettuce, olives, tomatoes, and avocado among the four tacos. Squeeze lime over the top prior to serving.

Blackberry Bbq Glazed Country-style Ribs

Servings: 2

Cooking Time: 40 Minutes

Ingredients:

- ½ cup + 2 tablespoons sherry or Madeira wine, divided
- 1 pound boneless country-style pork ribs
- salt and freshly ground black pepper
- 1 tablespoon Chinese 5-spice powder
- ¼ cup blackberry preserves
- ¼ cup hoisin sauce*
- 1 clove garlic, minced
- 1 generous tablespoon grated fresh ginger
- 2 scallions, chopped
- 1 tablespoon sesame seeds, toasted

Directions:

1. Preheat the air fryer to 330°F and pour ½ cup of the sherry into the bottom of the air fryer drawer.

2. Season the ribs with salt, pepper and the 5-spice powder.

3. Air-fry the ribs at 330°F for 20 minutes, turning them over halfway through the cooking time.

4. While the ribs are cooking, make the sauce. Combine the remaining sherry, blackberry preserves, hoisin sauce, garlic and ginger in a small saucepan. Bring to a simmer on the stovetop for a few minutes, until the sauce thickens.

5. When the time is up on the air fryer, turn the ribs over, pour a little sauce on the ribs and air-fry for another 10 minutes at 330°F. Turn the ribs over again, pour on more of the sauce and air-fry at 330°F for a final 10 minutes.

6. Let the ribs rest for at least 5 minutes before serving them warm with a little more glaze brushed on and the scallions and sesame seeds sprinkled on top.

California Burritos

Servings: 4

Cooking Time: 17 Minutes

Ingredients:

- 1 pound sirloin steak, sliced thin
- 1 teaspoon dried oregano
- 1 teaspoon ground cumin
- ½ teaspoon garlic powder
- 16 tater tots
- ⅓ cup sour cream
- ½ lime, juiced
- 2 tablespoons hot sauce
- 1 large avocado, pitted
- 1 teaspoon salt, divided
- 4 large (8- to 10-inch) flour tortillas
- ½ cup shredded cheddar cheese or Monterey jack
- 2 tablespoons avocado oil

Directions:

1. Preheat the air fryer to 380°F.

2. Season the steak with oregano, cumin, and garlic powder. Place the steak on one side of the air fryer and the tater tots on the other side. (It's okay for them to touch, because the flavors will all come together in the burrito.) Cook for 8 minutes, toss, and cook an additional 4 to 6 minutes.

3. Meanwhile, in a small bowl, stir together the sour cream, lime juice, and hot sauce.

4. In another small bowl, mash together the avocado and season with ½ teaspoon of the salt, to taste.

5. To assemble the burrito, lay out the tortillas, equally divide the meat amongst the tortillas. Season the steak equally with the remaining ½ teaspoon salt. Then layer the mashed avocado and sour cream mixture on top. Top each tortilla with 4 tater tots and finish each with 2 tablespoons cheese. Roll up the sides and, while holding in the sides, roll up the burrito. Place the burritos in the air fryer basket and brush with avocado oil (working in batches as needed); cook for 3 minutes or until lightly golden on the outside.

Baby Back Ribs

Servings: 4

Cooking Time: 36 Minutes

Ingredients:

- 2¼ pounds Pork baby back rib rack(s)
- 1 tablespoon Dried barbecue seasoning blend or rub (gluten-free, if a concern)
- 1 cup Water
- 3 tablespoons Purchased smooth barbecue sauce (gluten-free, if a concern)

Directions:

1. Preheat the air fryer to 350°F .

2. Cut the racks into 4- to 5-bone sections, about two sections for the small batch, three for the medium, and four for the large. Sprinkle both sides of these sections with the seasoning blend.

3. Pour the water into the bottom of the air-fryer drawer or into a tray placed under the rack. (The rack cannot then sit in water—adjust the amount of water for your machine.) Set the rib sections in the basket so that they're not touching. Air-fry for 30 minutes, turning once.

4. If using a tray with water, check it a couple of times to make sure it still has water in it or hasn't overflowed from the rendered fat.

5. Brush half the barbecue sauce on the exposed side of the ribs. Air-fry undisturbed for 3 minutes. Turn the racks over (but make sure they're still not touching), brush with the remaining sauce, and air-fry undisturbed for 3 minutes more, or until sizzling and brown.

6. Use kitchen tongs to transfer the racks to a cutting board. Let stand for 5 minutes, then slice between the bones to serve.

City "chicken"

Servings: 3

Cooking Time: 10 Minutes

Ingredients:

- 1 pound Pork tenderloin, cut into 2-inch cubes
- ½ cup All-purpose flour or tapioca flour
- 1 Large egg(s)
- 1 teaspoon Dried poultry seasoning blend
- 1¼ cups Plain panko bread crumbs (gluten-free, if a concern)
- Vegetable oil spray

Directions:

1. Preheat the air fryer to 350°F .

2. Thread 3 or 4 pieces of pork on a 4-inch bamboo skewer. You'll need 2 or 3 skewers for a small batch, 3 or 4 for a medium, and up to 6 for a large batch.

3. Set up and fill three shallow soup plates or small pie plates on your counter: one for the flour; one for the egg(s), beaten with the poultry seasoning until foamy; and one for the bread crumbs.

4. Dip and roll one skewer into the flour, coating all sides of the meat. Gently shake off any excess flour, then dip and roll the skewer in the egg mixture. Let any excess egg mixture slip back into the rest, then set the skewer in the bread crumbs and roll it around, pressing gently, until the exterior surfaces of the meat are evenly coated. Generously coat the meat on the skewer with vegetable oil spray. Set aside and continue dredging, dipping, coating, and spraying the remaining skewers.

5. Set the skewers in the basket in one layer and air-fry undisturbed for 10 minutes, or until brown and crunchy.

6. Use kitchen tongs to transfer the skewers to a wire rack. Cool for a minute or two before serving.

Venison Backstrap

Servings: 4

Cooking Time: 10 Minutes

Ingredients:

- 2 eggs
- ¼ cup milk
- 1 cup whole wheat flour
- ½ teaspoon salt
- ¼ teaspoon pepper
- 1 pound venison backstrap, sliced
- salt and pepper
- oil for misting or cooking spray

Directions:

1. Beat together eggs and milk in a shallow dish.
2. In another shallow dish, combine the flour, salt, and pepper. Stir to mix well.
3. Sprinkle venison steaks with additional salt and pepper to taste. Dip in flour, egg wash, then in flour again, pressing in coating.
4. Spray steaks with oil or cooking spray on both sides.
5. Cooking in 2 batches, place steaks in the air fryer basket in a single layer. Cook at 360°F for 8minutes. Spray with oil, turn over, and spray other side. Cook for 2 minutes longer, until coating is crispy brown and meat is done to your liking.
6. Repeat to cook remaining venison.

Stuffed Bell Peppers

Servings: 4

Cooking Time: 10 Minutes

Ingredients:

- ¼ pound lean ground pork
- ¾ pound lean ground beef
- ¼ cup onion, minced
- 1 15-ounce can Red Gold crushed tomatoes
- 1 teaspoon Worcestershire sauce
- 1 teaspoon barbeque seasoning
- 1 teaspoon honey
- ½ teaspoon dried basil
- ½ cup cooked brown rice
- ½ teaspoon garlic powder
- ½ teaspoon oregano
- ½ teaspoon salt
- 2 small bell peppers

Directions:

1. Place pork, beef, and onion in air fryer baking pan and cook at 360°F for 5minutes.

2. Stir to break apart chunks and cook 3 more minutes. Continue cooking and stirring in 2-minute intervals until meat is well done. Remove from pan and drain.

3. In a small saucepan, combine the tomatoes, Worcestershire, barbeque seasoning, honey, and basil. Stir well to mix in honey and seasonings.

4. In a large bowl, combine the cooked meat mixture, rice, garlic powder, oregano, and salt. Add ¼ cup of the seasoned crushed tomatoes. Stir until well mixed.

5. Cut peppers in half and remove stems and seeds.

6. Stuff each pepper half with one fourth of the meat mixture.

7. Place the peppers in air fryer basket and cook for 10 minutes, until peppers are crisp tender.

8. Heat remaining tomato sauce. Serve peppers with warm sauce spooned over top.

Bacon, Blue Cheese And Pear Stuffed Pork Chops

Servings: 3 Cooking Time: 24 Minutes

Ingredients:

- 4 slices bacon, chopped
- 1 tablespoon butter
- ½ cup finely diced onion
- ⅓ cup chicken stock
- 1½ cups seasoned stuffing cubes
- 1 egg, beaten
- ½ teaspoon dried thyme
- ½ teaspoon salt
- ⅛ teaspoon black pepper
- 1 pear, finely diced
- ⅓ cup crumbled blue cheese
- 3 boneless center-cut pork chops (2-inch thick)
- olive oil
- salt and freshly ground black pepper

Directions:

1. Preheat the air fryer to 400°F.

2. Place the bacon into the air fryer basket and air-fry for 6 minutes, stirring halfway through the cooking time. Remove the bacon and set it aside on a paper towel. Pour out the grease from the bottom of the air fryer.

3. To make the stuffing, melt the butter in a medium saucepan over medium heat on the stovetop. Add the onion and sauté for a few minutes, until it starts to soften. Add the chicken stock and simmer for 1 minute. Remove the pan from the heat and add the stuffing cubes. Stir until the stock has been absorbed. Add the egg, dried thyme, salt and freshly ground black pepper, and stir until combined. Fold in the diced pear and crumbled blue cheese.

4. Place the pork chops on a cutting board. Using the palm of your hand to hold the chop flat and steady, slice into the side of the pork chop to make a pocket in the center of the chop. Leave about an inch of chop uncut and make sure you don't cut all the way through the pork chop. Brush both sides of the pork chops with olive oil and season with salt and freshly ground black pepper. Stuff each pork chop with a third of the stuffing, packing the stuffing tightly inside the pocket.

5. Preheat the air fryer to 360°F.

6. Spray or brush the sides of the air fryer basket with oil. Place the pork chops in the air fryer basket with the open stuffed edge of the pork chop facing the outside edges of the basket.

7. Air-fry the pork chops for 18 minutes, turning the pork chops over halfway through the cooking time. When the chops are done, let them rest for 5 minutes and then transfer to a serving platter.

Crunchy Veal Cutlets

Servings: 2

Cooking Time: 5 Minutes

Ingredients:

- ½ cup All-purpose flour or tapioca flour
- 1 Large egg(s), well beaten
- ¾ cup Seasoned Italian-style dried bread crumbs (gluten-free, if a concern)
- 2 tablespoons Yellow cornmeal
- 4 Thinly pounded 2-ounce veal leg cutlets (less than ¼ inch thick)
- Olive oil spray

Directions:

1. Preheat the air fryer to 400°F.

2. Set up and fill three shallow soup plates or small pie plates on your counter: one for the flour; one for the egg(s); and one for the bread crumbs, whisked with the cornmeal until well combined.

3. Dredge a veal cutlet in the flour, coating it on both sides. Gently shake off any excess flour, then gently dip it in the beaten egg(s), coating both sides. Let the excess egg slip back into the rest. Dip the cutlet in the bread-crumb mixture, turning it several times and pressing gently to make an even coating on both sides. Coat it on both sides with olive oil spray, then set it aside and continue dredging and coating more cutlets.

4. When the machine is at temperature, set the cutlets in the basket so that they don't touch each other. Air-fry undisturbed for 5 minutes, or until crisp and brown. (If only some of the veal cutlets will fit in one layer for any selected batch—the sizes of air fryer baskets vary dramatically—work in batches as necessary.)

5. Use kitchen tongs to transfer the cutlets to a wire rack. Cool for only 1 to 2 minutes before serving.

Glazed Meatloaf

<table>
<tr><td>Servings: 4</td><td>Cooking Time: 35-55 Minutes</td></tr>
</table>

Ingredients:

- ½ cup Seasoned Italian-style panko bread crumbs (gluten-free, if a concern)
- ¼ cup Whole or low-fat milk
- 1 pound Lean ground beef
- 1 pound Bulk mild Italian sausage meat (gluten-free, if a concern)
- 1 Large egg(s), well beaten
- 1 teaspoon Dried thyme
- 1 teaspoon Onion powder
- 1 teaspoon Garlic powder
- Vegetable oil spray
- 1 tablespoon Ketchup (gluten-free, if a concern)
- 1 tablespoon Hoisin sauce (see here; gluten-free, if a concern)
- 2 teaspoons Pickle brine, preferably from a jar of jalapeño rings (gluten-free, if a concern)

Directions:

1. Pour the bread crumbs into a large bowl, add the milk, stir gently, and soak for 10 minutes.

2. Preheat the air fryer to 350°F .

3. Add the ground beef, Italian sausage meat, egg(s), thyme, onion powder, and garlic powder to the bowl with the bread crumbs. Blend gently until well combined. (Clean, dry hands work best!) Form this mixture into an oval loaf about 2 inches tall (its length will vary depending on the amount of ingredients) but with a flat bottom. Generously coat the top, bottom, and all sides of the loaf with vegetable oil spray.

4. Use a large, nonstick-safe spatula or perhaps silicone baking mitts to transfer the loaf to the basket. Air-fry undisturbed for 30 minutes for a small meatloaf, 40 minutes for a medium one, or 50 minutes for a large, until an instant-read meat thermometer inserted into the center of the loaf registers 165°F.

5. Whisk the ketchup, hoisin, and pickle brine in a small bowl until smooth. Brush this over the top and sides of the meatloaf and continue air-frying undisturbed for 5 minutes, or until the glaze has browned a bit. Use that same spatula or those same baking mitts to transfer the meatloaf to a cutting board. Cool for 10 minutes before slicing.

Bread And Breakfast

Quesadillas

Servings: 4

Cooking Time: 12 Minutes

Ingredients:

- 4 eggs
- 2 tablespoons skim milk
- salt and pepper
- oil for misting or cooking spray
- 4 flour tortillas
- 4 tablespoons salsa
- 2 ounces Cheddar cheese, grated
- ½ small avocado, peeled and thinly sliced

Directions:

1. Preheat air fryer to 270°F.
2. Beat together eggs, milk, salt, and pepper.
3. Spray a 6 x 6-inch air fryer baking pan lightly with cooking spray and add egg mixture.
4. Cook 9minutes, stirring every 1 to 2minutes, until eggs are scrambled to your liking. Remove and set aside.
5. Spray one side of each tortilla with oil or cooking spray. Flip over.
6. Divide eggs, salsa, cheese, and avocado among the tortillas, covering only half of each tortilla.
7. Fold each tortilla in half and press down lightly.
8. Place 2 tortillas in air fryer basket and cook at 390°F for 3minutes or until cheese melts and outside feels slightly crispy. Repeat with remaining two tortillas.
9. Cut each cooked tortilla into halves or thirds.

Scones

Servings: 9

Cooking Time: 8 Minutes Per Batch

Ingredients:

- 2 cups self-rising flour, plus ¼ cup for kneading
- ⅓ cup granulated sugar
- ¼ cup butter, cold
- 1 cup milk

Directions:

1. Preheat air fryer at 360°F.

2. In large bowl, stir together flour and sugar.

3. Cut cold butter into tiny cubes, and stir into flour mixture with fork.

4. Stir in milk until soft dough forms.

5. Sprinkle ¼ cup of flour onto wax paper and place dough on top. Knead lightly by folding and turning the dough about 6 to 8 times.

6. Pat dough into a 6 x 6-inch square.

7. Cut into 9 equal squares.

8. Place all squares in air fryer basket or as many as will fit in a single layer, close together but not touching.

9. Cook at 360°F for 8minutes. When done, scones will be lightly browned on top and will spring back when pressed gently with a dull knife.

10. Repeat steps 8 and 9 to cook remaining scones.

Fried Pb&j

Servings: 4

Cooking Time: 8 Minutes

Ingredients:

- ½ cup cornflakes, crushed
- ¼ cup shredded coconut
- 8 slices oat nut bread or any whole-grain, oversize bread
- 6 tablespoons peanut butter
- 2 medium bananas, cut into ½-inch-thick slices
- 6 tablespoons pineapple preserves
- 1 egg, beaten
- oil for misting or cooking spray

Directions:

1. Preheat air fryer to 360°F.

2. In a shallow dish, mix together the cornflake crumbs and coconut.

3. For each sandwich, spread one bread slice with 1½ tablespoons of peanut butter. Top with banana slices. Spread another bread slice with 1½ tablespoons of preserves. Combine to make a sandwich.

4. Using a pastry brush, brush top of sandwich lightly with beaten egg. Sprinkle with about 1½ tablespoons of crumb coating, pressing it in to make it stick. Spray with oil.

5. Turn sandwich over and repeat to coat and spray the other side.

6. Cooking 2 at a time, place sandwiches in air fryer basket and cook for 6 to 7minutes or until coating is golden brown and crispy. If sandwich doesn't brown enough, spray with a little more oil and cook at 390°F for another minute.

7. Cut cooked sandwiches in half and serve warm.

Broccoli Cornbread

Servings: 6

Cooking Time: 18 Minutes

Ingredients:

- 1 cup frozen chopped broccoli, thawed and drained
- ¼ cup cottage cheese
- 1 egg, beaten
- 2 tablespoons minced onion
- 2 tablespoons melted butter
- ½ cup flour
- ½ cup yellow cornmeal
- 1 teaspoon baking powder
- ½ teaspoon salt
- ¼ cup milk, plus 2 tablespoons
- cooking spray

Directions:

1. Place thawed broccoli in colander and press with a spoon to squeeze out excess moisture.
2. Stir together all ingredients in a large bowl.
3. Spray 6 x 6-inch baking pan with cooking spray.
4. Spread batter in pan and cook at 330°F for 18 minutes or until cornbread is lightly browned and loaf starts to pull away from sides of pan.

Soft Pretzels

Servings: 12   Cooking Time: 6 Minutes

Ingredients:

- 2 teaspoons yeast
- 1 cup water, warm
- 1 teaspoon sugar
- 1 teaspoon salt
- 2½ cups all-purpose flour
- 2 tablespoons butter, melted
- 1 cup boiling water
- 1 tablespoon baking soda
- coarse sea salt
- melted butter

Directions:

1. Combine the yeast and water in a small bowl. Combine the sugar, salt and flour in the bowl of a stand mixer. With the mixer running and using the dough hook, drizzle in the yeast mixture and melted butter and knead dough until smooth and elastic – about 10 minutes. Shape into a ball and let the dough rise for 1 hour.

2. Punch the dough down to release any air and decide what size pretzels you want to make.

3. a. To make large pretzels, divide the dough into 12 portions.

4. b. To make medium sized pretzels, divide the dough into 24 portions.

5. c. To make mini pretzel knots, divide the dough into 48 portions.

6. Roll each portion into a skinny rope using both hands on the counter and rolling from the center to the ends of the rope. Spin the rope into a pretzel shape (or tie the rope into a knot) and place the tied pretzels on a parchment lined baking sheet.

7. Preheat the air fryer to 350°F.

8. Combine the boiling water and baking soda in a shallow bowl and whisk to dissolve (this mixture will bubble, but it will settle down). Let the water cool so that you can put your hands in it. Working in batches, dip the pretzels (top side down) into the baking soda-water mixture and let them soak for 30 seconds to a minute. (This step is what gives pretzels their texture and helps them to brown faster.) Then, remove the pretzels carefully and return them (top side up) to the baking sheet. Sprinkle the coarse salt on the top.

9. Air-fry in batches for 3 minutes per side. When the pretzels are finished, brush them generously with the melted butter and enjoy them warm with some spicy mustard.

Pancake Muffins

<table>
<tr><td>Servings: 4</td><td>Cooking Time: 8 Minutes</td></tr>
</table>

Ingredients:

- 1 cup flour
- 2 tablespoons sugar (optional)
- ½ teaspoon baking soda
- 1 teaspoon baking powder
- ¼ teaspoon salt
- 1 egg, beaten
- 1 cup buttermilk
- 2 tablespoons melted butter
- 1 teaspoon pure vanilla extract
- 24 foil muffin cups
- cooking spray
- Suggested Fillings
- 1 teaspoon of jelly or fruit preserves
- 1 tablespoon or less fresh blueberries; chopped fresh strawberries; chopped frozen cherries; dark chocolate chips; chopped walnuts, pecans, or other nuts; cooked, crumbled bacon or sausage

Directions:

1. In a large bowl, stir together flour, optional sugar, baking soda, baking powder, and salt.

2. In a small bowl, combine egg, buttermilk, butter, and vanilla. Mix well.

3. Pour egg mixture into dry ingredients and stir to mix well but don't overbeat.

4. Double up the muffin cups and remove the paper liners from the top cups. Spray the foil cups lightly with cooking spray.

5. Place 6 sets of muffin cups in air fryer basket. Pour just enough batter into each cup to cover the bottom. Sprinkle with desired filling. Pour in more batter to cover the filling and fill the cups about ¾ full.

6. Cook at 330°F for 8minutes.

7. Repeat steps 5 and 6 for the remaining 6 pancake muffins.

Garlic-cheese Biscuits

Servings: 8

Cooking Time: 8 Minutes

Ingredients:

- 1 cup self-rising flour
- 1 teaspoon garlic powder
- 2 tablespoons butter, diced
- 2 ounces sharp Cheddar cheese, grated
- ½ cup milk
- cooking spray

Directions:

1. Preheat air fryer to 330°F.
2. Combine flour and garlic in a medium bowl and stir together.
3. Using a pastry blender or knives, cut butter into dry ingredients.
4. Stir in cheese.
5. Add milk and stir until stiff dough forms.
6. If dough is too sticky to handle, stir in 1 or 2 more tablespoons of self-rising flour before shaping. Biscuits should be firm enough to hold their shape. Otherwise, they'll stick to the air fryer basket.
7. Divide dough into 8 portions and shape into 2-inch biscuits about ¾-inch thick.
8. Spray air fryer basket with nonstick cooking spray.
9. Place all 8 biscuits in basket and cook at 330°F for 8 minutes.

Classic Cinnamon Rolls

Servings: 4

Cooking Time: 6 Minutes

Ingredients:

- 1½ cups all-purpose flour
- 1 tablespoon granulated sugar
- 2 teaspoons baking powder
- ½ teaspoon salt
- 4 tablespoons butter, divided
- ½ cup buttermilk
- 2 tablespoons brown sugar
- 1 teaspoon cinnamon
- 1 cup powdered sugar
- 2 tablespoons milk

Directions:

1. Preheat the air fryer to 360°F.

2. In a large bowl, stir together the flour, sugar, baking powder, and salt. Cut in 3 tablespoons of the butter with a pastry blender or two knives until coarse crumbs remain. Stir in the buttermilk until a dough forms.

3. Place the dough onto a floured surface and roll out into a square shape about ½ inch thick.

4. Melt the remaining 1 tablespoon of butter in the microwave for 20 seconds. Using a pastry brush or your fingers, spread the melted butter onto the dough.

5. In a small bowl, mix together the brown sugar and cinnamon. Sprinkle the mixture across the surface of the dough. Roll the dough up, forming a long log. Using a pastry cutter or sharp knife, cut 10 cinnamon rolls.

6. Carefully place the cinnamon rolls into the air fryer basket. Then bake at 360°F for 6 minutes or until golden brown.

7. Meanwhile, in a small bowl, whisk together the powdered sugar and milk.

8. Plate the cinnamon rolls and drizzle the glaze over the surface before serving.

Peach Fritters

Servings: 8

Cooking Time: 6 Minutes

Ingredients:

- 1½ cups bread flour
- 1 teaspoon active dry yeast
- ¼ cup sugar
- ¼ teaspoon salt
- ½ cup warm milk
- ½ teaspoon vanilla extract
- 2 egg yolks
- 2 tablespoons melted butter
- 2 cups small diced peaches (fresh or frozen)
- 1 tablespoon butter
- 1 teaspoon ground cinnamon
- 1 to 2 tablespoons sugar
- Glaze
- ¾ cup powdered sugar
- 4 teaspoons milk

Directions:

1. Combine the flour, yeast, sugar and salt in a bowl. Add the milk, vanilla, egg yolks and melted butter and combine until the dough starts to come together. Transfer the dough to a floured surface and knead it by hand for 2 minutes. Shape the dough into a ball, place it in a large oiled bowl, cover with a clean kitchen towel and let the dough rise in a warm place for 1 to 1½ hours, or until the dough has doubled in size.

2. While the dough is rising, melt one tablespoon of butter in a medium saucepan on the stovetop. Add the diced peaches, cinnamon and sugar to taste. Cook the peaches for about 5 minutes, or until they soften. Set the peaches aside to cool.

3. When the dough has risen, transfer it to a floured surface and shape it into a 12-inch circle. Spread the peaches over half of the circle and fold the other half of the dough over the top. With a knife or a board scraper, score the dough by making slits in the dough in a diamond shape. Push the knife straight down into the dough and peaches, rather than slicing through. You should cut through the top layer of dough, but not the bottom. Roll the dough up into a log from one short end to the other. It should be roughly 8 inches long. Some of the peaches will be sticking out of the dough – don't worry, these are supposed to be a little random. Cut the log into 8 equal slices. Place the dough disks on a floured cookie sheet, cover with a clean kitchen towel and let rise in a warm place for 30 minutes.

4. Preheat the air fryer to 370°F.

5. Air-fry 2 or 3 fritters at a time at 370°F, for 3 minutes. Flip them over and continue to air-fry for another 2 to 3 minutes, until they are golden brown.

6. Combine the powdered sugar and milk together in a small bowl. Whisk vigorously until smooth. Allow the fritters to cool for at least 10 minutes and then brush the glaze over both the bottom and top of each one. Serve warm or at room temperature.

Apple Fritters

Servings: 6

Cooking Time: 12 Minutes

Ingredients:

- 1 cup all-purpose flour
- 1½ teaspoons baking powder
- ¼ teaspoon salt
- 2 tablespoon brown sugar
- 1 teaspoon vanilla extract
- ¾ cup plain Greek yogurt
- 1 tablespoon cinnamon
- 1 large Granny Smith apple, cored, peeled, and finely chopped
- ¼ cup chopped walnuts
- ½ cup powdered sugar
- 1 tablespoon milk

Directions:

1. Preheat the air fryer to 320°F.

2. In a medium bowl, combine the flour, baking powder, and salt.

3. In a large bowl, add the brown sugar, vanilla, yogurt, cinnamon, apples, and walnuts. Mix the dry ingredients into the wet, using your hands to combine, until all the ingredients are mixed together. Knead the mixture in the bowl about 4 times.

4. Lightly spray the air fryer basket with olive oil spray.

5. Divide the batter into 6 equally sized balls; then lightly flatten them and place inside the basket. Repeat until all the fritters are formed.

6. Place the basket in the air fryer and cook for 6 minutes, flip, and then cook another 6 minutes.

7. While the fritters are cooking, in a small bowl, mix the powdered sugar with the milk. Set aside.

8. When the cooking completes, remove the air fryer basket and allow the fritters to cool on a wire rack. Drizzle with the homemade glaze and serve.

Sweet-hot Pepperoni Pizza

Servings: 2

Cooking Time: 18 Minutes

Ingredients:

- 1 (6- to 8-ounce) pizza dough ball*
- olive oil
- ½ cup pizza sauce
- ¾ cup grated mozzarella cheese
- ½ cup thick sliced pepperoni
- ⅓ cup sliced pickled hot banana peppers
- ¼ teaspoon dried oregano
- 2 teaspoons honey

Directions:

1. Preheat the air fryer to 390°F.

2. Cut out a piece of aluminum foil the same size as the bottom of the air fryer basket. Brush the foil circle with olive oil. Shape the dough into a circle and place it on top of the foil. Dock the dough by piercing it several times with a fork. Brush the dough lightly with olive oil and transfer it into the air fryer basket with the foil on the bottom.

3. Air-fry the plain pizza dough for 6 minutes. Turn the dough over, remove the aluminum foil and brush again with olive oil. Air-fry for an additional 4 minutes.

4. Spread the pizza sauce on top of the dough and sprinkle the mozzarella cheese over the sauce. Top with the pepperoni, pepper slices and dried oregano. Lower the temperature of the air fryer to 350°F and cook for 8 minutes, until the cheese has melted and lightly browned. Transfer the pizza to a cutting board and drizzle with the honey. Slice and serve.

Egg And Sausage Crescent Rolls

Servings: 8

Cooking Time: 11 Minutes

Ingredients:

- 5 large eggs
- ¼ teaspoon black pepper
- ¼ teaspoon salt
- 1 tablespoon milk
- ¼ cup shredded cheddar cheese
- One 8-ounce package refrigerated crescent rolls
- 4 tablespoon pesto sauce
- 8 fully cooked breakfast sausage links, defrosted

Directions:

1. Preheat the air fryer to 320°F.

2. In a medium bowl, crack the eggs and whisk with the pepper, salt, and milk. Pour into a frying pan over medium heat and scramble. Just before the eggs are done, turn off the heat and add in the cheese. Continue to cook until the cheese has melted and the eggs are finished (about 5 minutes total). Remove from the heat.

3. Remove the crescent rolls from the package and press them flat onto a clean surface lightly dusted with flour. Add 1½ teaspoons of pesto sauce across the center of each roll. Place equal portions of eggs across all 8 rolls. Then top each roll with a sausage link and roll the dough up tight so it resembles the crescent-roll shape.

4. Lightly spray your air fryer basket with olive oil mist and place the rolls on top. Bake for 6 minutes or until the tops of the rolls are lightly browned.

5. Remove and let cool 3 to 5 minutes before serving.

Vegetarians Recipes

Corn And Pepper Jack Chile Rellenos With Roasted Tomato Sauce

Servings: 3   Cooking Time: 30 Minutes

Ingredients:

- 3 Poblano peppers
- 1 cup all-purpose flour*
- salt and freshly ground black pepper
- 2 eggs, lightly beaten
- 1 cup plain breadcrumbs*
- olive oil, in a spray bottle
- Sauce
- 2 cups cherry tomatoes
- 1 Jalapeño pepper, halved and seeded
- 1 clove garlic
- ¼ red onion, broken into large pieces
- 1 tablespoon olive oil
- salt, to taste
- 2 tablespoons chopped fresh cilantro
- Filling
- olive oil
- ¼ red onion, finely chopped
- 1 teaspoon minced garlic
- 1 cup corn kernels, fresh or frozen
- 2 cups grated pepper jack cheese

Directions:

1. Start by roasting the peppers. Preheat the air fryer to 400°F. Place the peppers into the air fryer basket and air-fry at 400°F for 10 minutes, turning them over halfway through the cooking time. Remove the peppers from the basket and cover loosely with foil.

2. While the peppers are cooling, make the roasted tomato sauce. Place all sauce Ingredients except for the cilantro into the air fryer basket and air-fry at 400°F for 10 minutes, shaking the basket once or twice. When the sauce Ingredients have finished air-frying, transfer everything to a blender or food processor and blend or process to a smooth sauce, adding a little warm water to get the desired consistency. Season to taste with salt, add the cilantro and set aside.

3. While the sauce Ingredients are cooking in the air fryer, make the filling. Heat a skillet on the stovetop over medium heat. Add the olive oil and sauté the red onion and garlic for 4 to 5 minutes. Transfer the onion and garlic to a bowl, stir in the corn and cheese, and set aside.

4. Set up a dredging station with three shallow dishes. Place the flour, seasoned with salt and pepper, in the first shallow dish. Place the eggs in the second dish, and fill the third shallow dish with the breadcrumbs. When the peppers have cooled, carefully slice into one side of the pepper to create an opening. Pull the seeds out of the peppers and peel away the skins, trying not to tear the pepper. Fill each pepper with some of the corn and cheese filling and close the pepper up again by folding one side of the opening over the other. Carefully roll each pepper in the seasoned flour, then into the egg and

finally into the breadcrumbs to coat on all sides, trying not to let the pepper fall open. Spray the peppers on all sides with a little olive oil.

5.   Air-fry two peppers at a time at 350°F for 6 minutes. Turn the peppers over and air-fry for another 4 minutes. Serve the peppers warm on a bed of the roasted tomato sauce.

Spicy Vegetable And Tofu Shake Fry

Servings: 4

Cooking Time: 17 Minutes

Ingredients:

- 4 teaspoons canola oil, divided
- 2 tablespoons rice wine vinegar
- 1 tablespoon sriracha chili sauce
- ¼ cup soy sauce*
- ½ teaspoon toasted sesame oil
- 1 teaspoon minced garlic
- 1 tablespoon minced fresh ginger
- 8 ounces extra firm tofu
- ½ cup vegetable stock or water
- 1 tablespoon honey
- 1 tablespoon cornstarch
- ½ red onion, chopped
- 1 red or yellow bell pepper, chopped
- 1 cup green beans, cut into 2-inch lengths
- 4 ounces mushrooms, sliced
- 2 scallions, sliced
- 2 tablespoons fresh cilantro leaves
- 2 teaspoons toasted sesame seeds

Directions:

1.   Combine 1 tablespoon of the oil, vinegar, sriracha sauce, soy sauce, sesame oil, garlic and ginger in a small bowl. Cut the tofu into bite-sized cubes and toss the tofu in with the marinade while you prepare the other vegetables. When you are ready to start cooking, remove the tofu from the marinade and set it aside. Add the water, honey and cornstarch to the marinade and bring to a simmer on the stovetop, just until the sauce thickens. Set the sauce aside.

2.   Preheat the air fryer to 400°F.

3.   Toss the onion, pepper, green beans and mushrooms in a bowl with a little canola oil and season with salt. Air-fry at 400°F for 11 minutes, shaking the basket and tossing the vegetables every few minutes. When the vegetables are cooked to your preferred doneness, remove them from the air fryer and set aside.

4.   Add the tofu to the air fryer basket and air-fry at 400°F for 6 minutes, shaking the basket a few times during the cooking process. Add the vegetables back to the basket and air-fry for another minute. Transfer the vegetables and tofu to a large bowl, add the scallions and cilantro leaves and toss with the sauce. Serve over rice with sesame seeds sprinkled on top.

Roasted Vegetable, Brown Rice And Black Bean Burrito

Servings: 2

Cooking Time: 20 Minutes

Ingredients:

- ½ zucchini, sliced ¼-inch thick
- ½ red onion, sliced
- 1 yellow bell pepper, sliced
- 2 teaspoons olive oil
- salt and freshly ground black pepper
- 2 burrito size flour tortillas
- 1 cup grated pepper jack cheese
- ½ cup cooked brown rice
- ½ cup canned black beans, drained and rinsed
- ¼ teaspoon ground cumin
- 1 tablespoon chopped fresh cilantro
- fresh salsa, guacamole and sour cream, for serving

Directions:

1. Preheat the air fryer to 400°F.

2. Toss the vegetables in a bowl with the olive oil, salt and freshly ground black pepper. Air-fry at 400°F for 12 to 15 minutes, shaking the basket a few times during the cooking process. The vegetables are done when they are cooked to your liking.

3. In the meantime, start building the burritos. Lay the tortillas out on the counter. Sprinkle half of the cheese in the center of the tortillas. Combine the rice, beans, cumin and cilantro in a bowl, season to taste with salt and freshly ground black pepper and then divide the mixture between the two tortillas. When the vegetables have finished cooking, transfer them to the two tortillas, placing the vegetables on top of the rice and beans. Sprinkle the remaining cheese on top and then roll the burritos up, tucking in the sides of the tortillas as you roll. Brush or spray the outside of the burritos with olive oil and transfer them to the air fryer.

4. Air-fry at 360°F for 8 minutes, turning them over when there are about 2 minutes left. The burritos will have slightly brown spots, but will still be pliable.

5. Serve with some fresh salsa, guacamole and sour cream.

Cheese Ravioli

Servings: 4

Cooking Time: 9 Minutes

Ingredients:

- 1 egg
- ¼ cup milk
- 1 cup breadcrumbs
- 2 teaspoons Italian seasoning
- ⅛ teaspoon ground rosemary
- ¼ teaspoon basil
- ¼ teaspoon parsley
- 9-ounce package uncooked cheese ravioli
- ¼ cup flour
- oil for misting or cooking spray

Directions:

1. Preheat air fryer to 390°F.
2. In a medium bowl, beat together egg and milk.
3. In a large plastic bag, mix together the breadcrumbs, Italian seasoning, rosemary, basil, and parsley.
4. Place all the ravioli and the flour in a bag or a bowl with a lid and shake to coat.
5. Working with a handful at a time, drop floured ravioli into egg wash. Remove ravioli, letting excess drip off, and place in bag with breadcrumbs.
6. When all ravioli are in the breadcrumbs' bag, shake well to coat all pieces.
7. Dump enough ravioli into air fryer basket to form one layer. Mist with oil or cooking spray. Dump the remaining ravioli on top of the first layer and mist with oil.
8. Cook for 5minutes. Shake well and spray with oil. Break apart any ravioli stuck together and spray any spots you missed the first time.
9. Cook 4 minutes longer, until ravioli puff up and are crispy golden brown.

Mexican Twice Air-fried Sweet Potatoes

Servings: 2   Cooking Time: 42 Minutes

Ingredients:

- 2 large sweet potatoes
- olive oil
- salt and freshly ground black pepper
- ⅓ cup diced red onion
- ⅓ cup diced red bell pepper
- ½ cup canned black beans, drained and rinsed
- ½ cup corn kernels, fresh or frozen
- ½ teaspoon chili powder
- 1½ cups grated pepper jack cheese, divided
- Jalapeño peppers, sliced

Directions:

1. Preheat the air fryer to 400°F.

2. Rub the outside of the sweet potatoes with olive oil and season with salt and freshly ground black pepper. Transfer the potatoes into the air fryer basket and air-fry at 400°F for 30 minutes, rotating the potatoes a few times during the cooking process.

3. While the potatoes are air-frying, start the potato filling. Preheat a large sauté pan over medium heat on the stovetop. Add the onion and pepper and sauté for a few minutes, until the vegetables start to soften. Add the black beans, corn, and chili powder and sauté for another 3 minutes. Set the mixture aside.

4. Remove the sweet potatoes from the air fryer and let them rest for 5 minutes. Slice off one inch of the flattest side of both potatoes. Scrape the potato flesh out of the potatoes, leaving half an inch of potato flesh around the edge of the potato. Place all the potato flesh into a large bowl and mash it with a fork. Add the black bean mixture and 1 cup of the pepper jack cheese to the mashed sweet potatoes. Season with salt and freshly ground black pepper and mix well. Stuff the hollowed out potato shells with the black bean and sweet potato mixture, mounding the filling high in the potatoes.

5. Transfer the stuffed potatoes back into the air fryer basket and air-fry at 370°F for 10 minutes. Sprinkle the remaining cheese on top of each stuffed potato, lower the heat to 340°F and air-fry for an additional 2 minutes to melt the cheese. Top with a couple slices of Jalapeño pepper and serve warm with a green salad.

Veggie Fried Rice

Servings: 4

Cooking Time: 25 Minutes

Ingredients:

- 1 cup cooked brown rice
- ⅓ cup chopped onion
- ½ cup chopped carrots
- ½ cup chopped bell peppers
- ½ cup chopped broccoli florets
- 3 tablespoons low-sodium soy sauce
- 1 tablespoon sesame oil
- 1 teaspoon ground ginger
- 1 teaspoon ground garlic powder
- ½ teaspoon black pepper
- ⅛ teaspoon salt
- 2 large eggs

Directions:

1. Preheat the air fryer to 370°F.

2. In a large bowl, mix together the brown rice, onions, carrots, bell pepper, and broccoli.

3. In a small bowl, whisk together the soy sauce, sesame oil, ginger, garlic powder, pepper, salt, and eggs.

4. Pour the egg mixture into the rice and vegetable mixture and mix together.

5. Liberally spray a 7-inch springform pan (or compatible air fryer dish) with olive oil. Add the rice mixture to the pan and cover with aluminum foil.

6. Place a metal trivet into the air fryer basket and set the pan on top. Cook for 15 minutes. Carefully remove the pan from basket, discard the foil, and mix the rice. Return the rice to the air fryer basket, turning down the temperature to 350°F and cooking another 10 minutes.

7. Remove and let cool 5 minutes. Serve warm.

Black Bean Empanadas

Servings: 12	Cooking Time: 35 Minutes

Ingredients:

- 1½ cups all-purpose flour
- 1 cup whole-wheat flour
- 1 teaspoon salt
- ½ cup cold unsalted butter
- 1 egg
- ½ cup milk
- One 14.5-ounce can black beans, drained and rinsed
- ¼ cup chopped cilantro
- 1 cup shredded purple cabbage
- 1 cup shredded Monterey jack cheese
- ¼ cup salsa

Directions:

1. In a food processor, place the all-purpose flour, whole-wheat flour, salt, and butter into processor and process for 2 minutes, scraping down the sides of the food processor every 30 seconds. Add in the egg and blend for 30 seconds. Using the pulse button, add in the milk 1 tablespoon at a time, or until dough is moist enough to handle and be rolled into a ball. Let the dough rest at room temperature for 30 minutes.

2. Meanwhile, in a large bowl, mix together the black beans, cilantro, cabbage, Monterey Jack cheese, and salsa.

3. On a floured surface, cut the dough in half; then form a ball and cut each ball into 6 equal pieces, totaling 12 equal pieces. Work with one piece at a time, and cover the remaining dough with a towel.

4. Roll out a piece of dough into a 6-inch round, much like a tortilla, ¼ inch thick. Place 4 tablespoons of filling in the center of the round, and fold over to form a half-circle. Using a fork, crimp the edges together and pierce the top for air holes. Repeat with the remaining dough and filling.

5. Preheat the air fryer to 350°F.

6. Working in batches, place 3 to 4 empanadas in the air fryer basket and spray with cooking spray. Cook for 4 minutes, flip over the empanadas and spray with cooking spray, and cook another 4 minutes.

Roasted Vegetable Stromboli

<table>
<tr><td>Servings: 2</td><td>Cooking Time: 29 Minutes</td></tr>
</table>

Ingredients:

- ½ onion, thinly sliced
- ½ red pepper, julienned
- ½ yellow pepper, julienned
- olive oil
- 1 small zucchini, thinly sliced
- 1 cup thinly sliced mushrooms
- 1½ cups chopped broccoli
- 1 teaspoon Italian seasoning
- salt and freshly ground black pepper
- ½ recipe of Blue Jean Chef Pizza dough (page 231) OR 1 (14-ounce) tube refrigerated pizza dough
- 2 cups grated mozzarella cheese
- ¼ cup grated Parmesan cheese
- ½ cup sliced black olives, optional
- dried oregano
- pizza or marinara sauce

Directions:

1. Preheat the air fryer to 400°F.

2. Toss the onions and peppers with a little olive oil and air-fry the vegetables for 7 minutes, shaking the basket once or twice while the vegetables cook. Add the zucchini, mushrooms, broccoli and Italian seasoning to the basket. Add a little more olive oil and season with salt and freshly ground black pepper. Air-fry for an additional 7 minutes, shaking the basket halfway through. Let the vegetables cool slightly while you roll out the pizza dough.

3. On a lightly floured surface, roll or press the pizza dough out into a 13-inch by 11-inch rectangle, with the long side closest to you. Sprinkle half of the mozzarella and Parmesan cheeses over the dough leaving an empty 1-inch border from the edge farthest away from you. Spoon the roasted vegetables over the cheese, sprinkle the olives over everything and top with the remaining cheese.

4. Start rolling the stromboli away from you and toward the empty border. Make sure the filling stays tightly tucked inside the roll. Finally, tuck the ends of the dough in and pinch the seam shut. Place the seam side down and shape the stromboli into a U-shape to fit into the air fryer basket. Cut 4 small slits with the tip of a sharp knife evenly in the top of the dough, lightly brush the stromboli with a little oil and sprinkle with some dried oregano.

5. Preheat the air fryer to 360°F.

6. Spray or brush the air fryer basket with oil and transfer the U-shaped stromboli to the air fryer basket. Air-fry for 15 minutes, flipping the stromboli over after the first 10 minutes. (Use a plate to invert the Stromboli out of the air fryer basket and then slide it back into the basket off the plate.)

7. To remove, carefully flip the stromboli over onto a cutting board. Let it rest for a couple of minutes before serving. Cut it into 2-inch slices and serve with pizza or marinara sauce.

Tacos

Servings: 24

Cooking Time: 8 Minutes Per Batch

Ingredients:

- 1 24-count package 4-inch corn tortillas
- 1½ cups refried beans (about ¾ of a 15-ounce can)
- 4 ounces sharp Cheddar cheese, grated
- ½ cup salsa
- oil for misting or cooking spray

Directions:

1. Preheat air fryer to 390°F.
2. Wrap refrigerated tortillas in damp paper towels and microwave for 30 to 60 seconds to warm. If necessary, rewarm tortillas as you go to keep them soft enough to fold without breaking.
3. Working with one tortilla at a time, top with 1 tablespoon of beans, 1 tablespoon of grated cheese, and 1 teaspoon of salsa. Fold over and press down very gently on the center. Press edges firmly all around to seal. Spray both sides with oil or cooking spray.
4. Cooking in two batches, place half the tacos in the air fryer basket. To cook 12 at a time, you may need to stand them upright and lean some against the sides of basket. It's okay if they're crowded as long as you leave a little room for air to circulate around them.
5. Cook for 8 minutes or until golden brown and crispy.
6. Repeat steps 4 and 5 to cook remaining tacos.

Eggplant Parmesan

Servings: 4

Cooking Time: 8 Minutes Per Batch

Ingredients:

- 1 medium eggplant, 6–8 inches long
- salt
- 1 large egg
- 1 tablespoon water
- ⅔ cup panko breadcrumbs
- ⅓ cup grated Parmesan cheese, plus more for serving
- 1 tablespoon Italian seasoning
- ¾ teaspoon oregano
- oil for misting or cooking spray
- 1 24-ounce jar marinara sauce
- 8 ounces spaghetti, cooked
- pepper

Directions:

1. Preheat air fryer to 390°F.
2. Leaving peel intact, cut eggplant into 8 round slices about ¾-inch thick. Salt to taste.
3. Beat egg and water in a shallow dish.
4. In another shallow dish, combine panko, Parmesan, Italian seasoning, and oregano.
5. Dip eggplant slices in egg wash and then crumbs, pressing lightly to coat.
6. Mist slices with oil or cooking spray.
7. Place 4 eggplant slices in air fryer basket and cook for 8 minutes, until brown and crispy.
8. While eggplant is cooking, heat marinara sauce.
9. Repeat step 7 to cook remaining eggplant slices.
10. To serve, place cooked spaghetti on plates and top with marinara and eggplant slices. At the table, pass extra Parmesan cheese and freshly ground black pepper.

Stuffed Zucchini Boats

Servings: 2

Cooking Time: 20 Minutes

Ingredients:

- olive oil
- ½ cup onion, finely chopped
- 1 clove garlic, finely minced
- ½ teaspoon dried oregano
- ¼ teaspoon dried thyme
- ¾ cup couscous
- 1½ cups chicken stock, divided
- 1 tomato, seeds removed and finely chopped
- ½ cup coarsely chopped Kalamata olives
- ½ cup grated Romano cheese
- ¼ cup pine nuts, toasted
- 1 tablespoon chopped fresh parsley
- 1 teaspoon salt
- freshly ground black pepper
- 1 egg, beaten
- 1 cup grated mozzarella cheese, divided
- 2 thick zucchini

Directions:

1. Preheat a sauté pan on the stovetop over medium-high heat. Add the olive oil and sauté the onion until it just starts to soften–about 4 minutes. Stir in the garlic, dried oregano and thyme. Add the couscous and sauté for just a minute. Add 1¼ cups of the chicken stock and simmer over low heat for 3 to 5 minutes, until liquid has been absorbed and the couscous is soft. Remove the pan from heat and set it aside to cool slightly.

2. Fluff the couscous and add the tomato, Kalamata olives, Romano cheese, pine nuts, parsley, salt and pepper. Mix well. Add the remaining chicken stock, the egg and ½ cup of the mozzarella cheese. Stir to ensure everything is combined.

3. Cut each zucchini in half lengthwise. Then, trim each half of the zucchini into four 5-inch lengths. (Save the trimmed ends of the zucchini for another use.) Use a spoon to scoop out the center of the zucchini, leaving some flesh around the sides. Brush both sides of the zucchini with olive oil and season the cut side with salt and pepper.

4. Preheat the air fryer to 380°F.

5. Divide the couscous filling between the four zucchini boats. Use your hands to press the filling together and fill the inside of the zucchini. The filling should be mounded into the boats and rounded on top.

6. Transfer the zucchini boats to the air fryer basket and drizzle the stuffed zucchini boats with olive oil. Air-fry for 19 minutes. Then, sprinkle the remaining mozzarella cheese on top of the zucchini, pressing it down onto the filling lightly to prevent it from blowing around in the air fryer. Air-fry for one more minute to melt the cheese. Transfer the finished zucchini boats to a serving platter and garnish with the chopped parsley.

Vegetable Couscous

Servings: 4

Cooking Time: 10 Minutes

Ingredients:

- 4 ounces white mushrooms, sliced
- ½ medium green bell pepper, julienned
- 1 cup cubed zucchini
- ¼ small onion, slivered
- 1 stalk celery, thinly sliced
- ¼ teaspoon ground coriander
- ¼ teaspoon ground cumin
- salt and pepper
- 1 tablespoon olive oil
- Couscous
- ¾ cup uncooked couscous
- 1 cup vegetable broth or water
- ½ teaspoon salt (omit if using salted broth)

Directions:

1. Combine all vegetables in large bowl. Sprinkle with coriander, cumin, and salt and pepper to taste. Stir well, add olive oil, and stir again to coat vegetables evenly.

2. Place vegetables in air fryer basket and cook at 390°F for 5minutes. Stir and cook for 5 more minutes, until tender.

3. While vegetables are cooking, prepare the couscous: Place broth or water and salt in large saucepan. Heat to boiling, stir in couscous, cover, and remove from heat.

4. Let couscous sit for 5minutes, stir in cooked vegetables, and serve hot.

Desserts And Sweets

Puff Pastry Apples

Servings: 4   Cooking Time: 10 Minutes

Ingredients:

- 3 Rome or Gala apples, peeled
- 2 tablespoons sugar
- 1 teaspoon all-purpose flour
- 1 teaspoon ground cinnamon
- ⅛ teaspoon ground ginger
- pinch ground nutmeg
- 1 sheet puff pastry
- 1 tablespoon butter, cut into 4 pieces
- 1 egg, beaten
- vegetable oil
- vanilla ice cream (optional)
- caramel sauce (optional)

Directions:

1. Remove the core from the apple by cutting the four sides off the apple around the core. Slice the pieces of apple into thin half-moons, about ¼-inch thick. Combine the sugar, flour, cinnamon, ginger, and nutmeg in a large bowl. Add the apples to the bowl and gently toss until the apples are evenly coated with the spice mixture. Set aside.

2. Cut the puff pastry sheet into a 12-inch by 12-inch square. Then quarter the sheet into four 6-inch squares. Save any remaining pastry for decorating the apples at the end.

3. Divide the spiced apples between the four puff pastry squares, stacking the apples in the center of each square and placing them flat on top of each other in a circle. Top the apples with a piece of the butter.

4. Brush the four edges of the pastry with the egg wash. Bring the four corners of the pastry together, wrapping them around the apple slices and pinching them together at the top in the style of a "beggars purse" appetizer. Fold the ends of the pastry corners down onto the apple making them look like leaves. Brush the entire apple with the egg wash.

5. Using the leftover dough, make leaves to decorate the apples. Cut out 8 leaf shapes, about 1½-inches long, "drawing" the leaf veins on the pastry leaves with a paring knife. Place 2 leaves on the top of each apple, tucking the ends of the leaves under the pastry in the center of the apples. Brush the top of the leaves with additional egg wash. Sprinkle the entire apple with some granulated sugar.

6. Preheat the air fryer to 350°F.

7.   Spray or brush the inside of the air fryer basket with oil. Place the apples in the basket and air-fry for 6 minutes. Carefully turn the apples over – it's easiest to remove one apple, then flip the others over and finally return the last apple to the air fryer. Air-fry for an additional 4 minutes.

8.   Serve the puff pastry apples warm with vanilla ice cream and drizzle with some caramel sauce.

Blueberry Crisp

Servings: 6   Cooking Time: 13 Minutes

Ingredients:

- 3 cups Fresh or thawed frozen blueberries
- ⅓ cup Granulated white sugar
- 1 tablespoon Instant tapioca
- ⅓ cup All-purpose flour
- ⅓ cup Rolled oats (not quick-cooking or steel-cut)
- ⅓ cup Chopped walnuts or pecans
- ⅓ cup Packed light brown sugar
- 5 tablespoons plus 1 teaspoon (⅔ stick) Butter, melted and cooled
- ¾ teaspoon Ground cinnamon
- ¼ teaspoon Table salt

Directions:

1.   Preheat the air fryer to 400°F.

2.   Mix the blueberries, granulated white sugar, and instant tapioca in a 6-inch round cake pan for a small batch, a 7-inch round cake pan for a medium batch, or an 8-inch round cake pan for a large batch.

3.   When the machine is at temperature, set the cake pan in the basket and air-fry undisturbed for 5 minutes, or just until the blueberries begin to bubble.

4.   Meanwhile, mix the flour, oats, nuts, brown sugar, butter, cinnamon, and salt in a medium bowl until well combined.

5.   When the blueberries have begun to bubble, crumble this flour mixture evenly on top. Continue air-frying undisturbed for 8 minutes, or until the topping has browned a bit and the filling is bubbling.

6.   Use two hot pads or silicone baking mitts to transfer the cake pan to a wire rack. Cool for at least 10 minutes or to room temperature before serving.

Mixed Berry Hand Pies

Servings: 4

Cooking Time: 15 Minutes

Ingredients:

- ¾ cup sugar
- ½ teaspoon ground cinnamon
- 1 tablespoon cornstarch
- 1 cup blueberries
- 1 cup blackberries
- 1 cup raspberries, divided
- 1 teaspoon water
- 1 package refrigerated pie dough (or your own homemade pie dough)
- 1 egg, beaten

Directions:

1. Combine the sugar, cinnamon, and cornstarch in a small saucepan. Add the blueberries, blackberries, and ½ cup of the raspberries. Toss the berries gently to coat them evenly. Add the teaspoon of water to the saucepan and turn the stovetop on to medium-high heat, stirring occasionally. Once the berries break down, release their juice and start to simmer (about 5 minutes), simmer for another couple of minutes and then transfer the mixture to a bowl, stir in the remaining ½ cup of raspberries and let it cool.

2. Preheat the air fryer to 370°F.

3. Cut the pie dough into four 5-inch circles and four 6-inch circles.

4. Spread the 6-inch circles on a flat surface. Divide the berry filling between all four circles. Brush the perimeter of the dough circles with a little water. Place the 5-inch circles on top of the filling and press the perimeter of the dough circles together to seal. Roll the edges of the bottom circle up over the top circle to make a crust around the filling. Press a fork around the crust to make decorative indentations and to seal the crust shut. Brush the pies with egg wash and sprinkle a little sugar on top. Poke a small hole in the center of each pie with a paring knife to vent the dough.

5. Air-fry two pies at a time. Brush or spray the air fryer basket with oil and place the pies into the basket. Air-fry for 9 minutes. Turn the pies over and air-fry for another 6 minutes. Serve warm or at room temperature.

Almond-roasted Pears

Servings: 4

Cooking Time: 15 Minutes

Ingredients:

- Yogurt Topping
- 1 container vanilla Greek yogurt (5–6 ounces)
- ¼ teaspoon almond flavoring
- 2 whole pears
- ¼ cup crushed Biscoff cookies (approx. 4 cookies)
- 1 tablespoon sliced almonds
- 1 tablespoon butter

Directions:

1. Stir almond flavoring into yogurt and set aside while preparing pears.
2. Halve each pear and spoon out the core.
3. Place pear halves in air fryer basket.
4. Stir together the cookie crumbs and almonds. Place a quarter of this mixture into the hollow of each pear half.
5. Cut butter into 4 pieces and place one piece on top of crumb mixture in each pear.
6. Cook at 360°F for 15 minutes or until pears have cooked through but are still slightly firm.
7. Serve pears warm with a dollop of yogurt topping.

Vegan Brownie Bites

Servings: 10

Cooking Time: 8 Minutes

Ingredients:

- ⅔ cup walnuts
- ⅓ cup all-purpose flour
- ¼ cup dark cocoa powder
- ⅓ cup cane sugar
- ¼ teaspoon salt
- 2 tablespoons vegetable oil
- 1 teaspoon pure vanilla extract
- 1 tablespoon almond milk
- 1 tablespoon powdered sugar

Directions:

1. Preheat the air fryer to 350°F.

2. To a blender or food processor fitted with a metal blade, add the walnuts, flour, cocoa powder, sugar, and salt. Pulse until smooth, about 30 seconds. Add in the oil, vanilla, and milk and pulse until a dough is formed.

3. Remove the dough and place in a bowl. Form into 10 equal-size bites.

4. Liberally spray the metal trivet in the air fryer basket with olive oil mist. Place the brownie bites into the basket and cook for 8 minutes, or until the outer edges begin to slightly crack.

5. Remove the basket from the air fryer and let cool. Sprinkle the brownie bites with powdered sugar and serve.

Cherry Hand Pies

Servings: 8

Cooking Time: 8 Minutes

Ingredients:

- 4 cups frozen or canned pitted tart cherries (if using canned, drain and pat dry)
- 2 teaspoons lemon juice
- ½ cup sugar
- ¼ cup cornstarch
- 1 teaspoon vanilla extract
- 1 Basic Pie Dough (see the preceding recipe) or store-bought pie dough

Directions:

1. In a medium saucepan, place the cherries and lemon juice and cook over medium heat for 10 minutes, or until the cherries begin to break down.

2. In a small bowl, stir together the sugar and cornstarch. Pour the sugar mixture into the cherries, stirring constantly. Cook the cherry mixture over low heat for 2 to 3 minutes, or until thickened. Remove from the heat and stir in the vanilla extract. Allow the cherry mixture to cool to room temperature, about 30 minutes.

3. Meanwhile, bring the pie dough to room temperature. Divide the dough into 8 equal pieces. Roll out the dough to ¼-inch thickness in circles. Place ¼ cup filling in the center of each rolled dough. Fold the dough to create a half-circle. Using a fork, press around the edges to seal the hand pies. Pierce the top of the pie with a fork for steam release while cooking. Continue until 8 hand pies are formed.

4. Preheat the air fryer to 350°F.

5. Place a single layer of hand pies in the air fryer basket and spray with cooking spray. Cook for 8 to 10 minutes or until golden brown and cooked through.

Blueberry Cheesecake Tartlets

Servings: 9

Cooking Time: 6 Minutes

Ingredients:

- 8 ounces cream cheese, softened
- ¼ cup sugar
- 1 egg
- ½ teaspoon vanilla extract
- zest of 2 lemons, divided
- 9 mini graham cracker tartlet shells*
- 2 cups blueberries
- ½ teaspoon ground cinnamon
- juice of ½ lemon
- ¼ cup apricot preserves

Directions:

1. Preheat the air fryer to 330°F.

2. Combine the cream cheese, sugar, egg, vanilla and the zest of one lemon in a medium bowl and blend until smooth by hand or with an electric hand mixer. Pour the cream cheese mixture into the tartlet shells.

3. Air-fry 3 tartlets at a time at 330°F for 6 minutes, rotating them in the air fryer basket halfway through the cooking time.

4. Combine the blueberries, cinnamon, zest of one lemon and juice of half a lemon in a bowl. Melt the apricot preserves in the microwave or over low heat in a saucepan. Pour the apricot preserves over the blueberries and gently toss to coat.

5. Allow the cheesecakes to cool completely and then top each one with some of the blueberry mixture. Garnish the tartlets with a little sugared lemon peel and refrigerate until you are ready to serve.

Donut Holes

Servings: 13

Cooking Time: 12 Minutes

Ingredients:

- 6 tablespoons Granulated white sugar
- 1½ tablespoons Butter, melted and cooled
- 2 tablespoons (or 1 small egg, well beaten) Pasteurized egg substitute, such as Egg Beaters
- 6 tablespoons Regular or low-fat sour cream (not fat-free)
- ¾ teaspoon Vanilla extract
- 1⅔ cups All-purpose flour
- ¾ teaspoon Baking powder
- ¼ teaspoon Table salt
- Vegetable oil spray

Directions:

1. Preheat the air fryer to 350°F .

2. Whisk the sugar and melted butter in a medium bowl until well combined. Whisk in the egg substitute or egg , then the sour cream and vanilla until smooth. Remove the whisk and stir in the flour, baking powder, and salt with a wooden spoon just until a soft dough forms.

3. Use 2 tablespoons of this dough to create a ball between your clean palms. Set it aside and continue making balls: 8 more for the small batch, 12 more for the medium batch, or 17 more for the large one.

4. Coat the balls in the vegetable oil spray, then set them in the basket with as much air space between them as possible. Even a fraction of an inch will be enough, but they should not touch. Air-fry undisturbed for 12 minutes, or until browned and cooked through. A toothpick inserted into the center of a ball should come out clean.

5. Pour the contents of the basket onto a wire rack. Cool for at least 5 minutes before serving.

Cheesecake Wontons

Servings:16

Cooking Time: 6 Minutes

Ingredients:

- ¼ cup Regular or low-fat cream cheese (not fat-free)
- 2 tablespoons Granulated white sugar
- 1½ tablespoons Egg yolk
- ¼ teaspoon Vanilla extract
- ⅛ teaspoon Table salt
- 1½ tablespoons All-purpose flour
- 16 Wonton wrappers (vegetarian, if a concern)
- Vegetable oil spray

Directions:

1. Preheat the air fryer to 400°F.

2. Using a flatware fork, mash the cream cheese, sugar, egg yolk, and vanilla in a small bowl until smooth. Add the salt and flour and continue mashing until evenly combined.

3. Set a wonton wrapper on a clean, dry work surface so that one corner faces you (so that it looks like a diamond on your work surface). Set 1 teaspoon of the cream cheese mixture in the middle of the wrapper but just above a horizontal line that would divide the wrapper in half. Dip your clean finger in water and run it along the edges of the wrapper. Fold the corner closest to you up and over the filling, lining it up with the corner farthest from you, thereby making a stuffed triangle. Press gently to seal. Wet the two triangle tips nearest you, then fold them up and together over the filling. Gently press together to seal and fuse. Set aside and continue making more stuffed wontons, 11 more for the small batch, 15 more for the medium batch, or 23 more for the large one.

4. Lightly coat the stuffed wrappers on all sides with vegetable oil spray. Set them with the fused corners up in the basket with as much air space between them as possible. Air-fry undisturbed for 6 minutes, or until golden brown and crisp.

5. Gently dump the contents of the basket onto a wire rack. Cool for at least 5 minutes before serving.

Fried Banana S'mores

Servings: 4

Cooking Time: 6 Minutes

Ingredients:

- 4 bananas
- 3 tablespoons mini semi-sweet chocolate chips
- 3 tablespoons mini peanut butter chips
- 3 tablespoons mini marshmallows
- 3 tablespoons graham cracker cereal

Directions:

1. Preheat the air fryer to 400°F.

2. Slice into the un-peeled bananas lengthwise along the inside of the curve, but do not slice through the bottom of the peel. Open the banana slightly to form a pocket.

3. Fill each pocket with chocolate chips, peanut butter chips and marshmallows. Poke the graham cracker cereal into the filling.

4. Place the bananas in the air fryer basket, resting them on the side of the basket and each other to keep them upright with the filling facing up. Air-fry for 6 minutes, or until the bananas are soft to the touch, the peels have blackened and the chocolate and marshmallows have melted and toasted.

5. Let them cool for a couple of minutes and then simply serve with a spoon to scoop out the filling.

Keto Cheesecake Cups

Servings: 6

Cooking Time: 10 Minutes

Ingredients:

- 8 ounces cream cheese
- ¼ cup plain whole-milk Greek yogurt
- 1 large egg
- 1 teaspoon pure vanilla extract
- 3 tablespoons monk fruit sweetener
- ¼ teaspoon salt
- ½ cup walnuts, roughly chopped

Directions:

1. Preheat the air fryer to 315°F.

2. In a large bowl, use a hand mixer to beat the cream cheese together with the yogurt, egg, vanilla, sweetener, and salt. When combined, fold in the chopped walnuts.

3. Set 6 silicone muffin liners inside an air-fryer-safe pan. Note: This is to allow for an easier time getting the cheesecake bites in and out. If you don't have a pan, you can place them directly in the air fryer basket.

4. Evenly fill the cupcake liners with cheesecake batter.

5. Carefully place the pan into the air fryer basket and cook for about 10 minutes, or until the tops are lightly browned and firm.

6. Carefully remove the pan when done and place in the refrigerator for 3 hours to firm up before serving.

One-bowl Chocolate Buttermilk Cake

Servings: 6   Cooking Time: 16-20 Minutes

Ingredients:

- ¾ cup All-purpose flour
- ½ cup Granulated white sugar
- 3 tablespoons Unsweetened cocoa powder
- ½ teaspoon Baking soda
- ¼ teaspoon Table salt
- ½ cup Buttermilk
- 2 tablespoons Vegetable oil
- ¾ teaspoon Vanilla extract
- Baking spray (see here)

Directions:

1. Preheat the air fryer to 325°F (or 330°F, if that's the closest setting).

2. Stir the flour, sugar, cocoa powder, baking soda, and salt in a large bowl until well combined. Add the buttermilk, oil, and vanilla. Stir just until a thick, grainy batter forms.

3. Use the baking spray to generously coat the inside of a 6-inch round cake pan for a small batch, a 7-inch round cake pan for a medium batch, or an 8-inch round cake pan for a large batch. Scrape and spread the chocolate batter into this pan, smoothing the batter out to an even layer.

4. Set the pan in the basket and air-fry undisturbed for 16 minutes for a 6-inch layer, 18 minutes for a 7-inch layer, or 20 minutes for an 8-inch layer, or until a toothpick or cake tester inserted into the center of the cake comes out clean. Start checking it at the 14-minute mark to know where you are.

5. Use hot pads or silicone baking mitts to transfer the cake pan to a wire rack. Cool for 5 minutes. To unmold, set a cutting board over the baking pan and invert both the board and the pan. Lift the still-warm pan off the cake layer. Set the wire rack on top of the cake layer and invert all of it with the cutting board so that the cake layer is now right side up on the wire rack. Remove the cutting board and continue cooling the cake for at least 10 minutes or to room temperature, about 30 minutes, before slicing into wedges.

Fish And Seafood Recipes

Shrimp, Chorizo And Fingerling Potatoes

Servings: 4

Cooking Time: 16 Minutes

Ingredients:

- ½ red onion, chopped into 1-inch chunks
- 8 fingerling potatoes, sliced into 1-inch slices or halved lengthwise
- 1 teaspoon olive oil
- salt and freshly ground black pepper
- 8 ounces raw chorizo sausage, sliced into 1-inch chunks
- 16 raw large shrimp, peeled, deveined and tails removed
- 1 lime
- ¼ cup chopped fresh cilantro
- chopped orange zest (optional)

Directions:

1. Preheat the air fryer to 380°F.

2. Combine the red onion and potato chunks in a bowl and toss with the olive oil, salt and freshly ground black pepper.

3. Transfer the vegetables to the air fryer basket and air-fry for 6 minutes, shaking the basket a few times during the cooking process.

4. Add the chorizo chunks and continue to air-fry for another 5 minutes.

5. Add the shrimp, season with salt and continue to air-fry, shaking the basket every once in a while, for another 5 minutes.

6. Transfer the tossed shrimp, chorizo and potato to a bowl and squeeze some lime juice over the top to taste. Toss in the fresh cilantro, orange zest and a drizzle of olive oil, and season again to taste.

7. Serve with a fresh green salad.

Better Fish Sticks

Servings:3

Cooking Time: 8 Minutes

Ingredients:

- ¾ cup Seasoned Italian-style dried bread crumbs (gluten-free, if a concern)
- 3 tablespoons (about ½ ounce) Finely grated Parmesan cheese
- 10 ounces Skinless cod fillets, cut lengthwise into 1-inch-wide pieces
- 3 tablespoons Regular or low-fat mayonnaise (not fat-free; gluten-free, if a concern)
- Vegetable oil spray

Directions:

1. Preheat the air fryer to 400°F.

2. Mix the bread crumbs and grated Parmesan in a shallow soup bowl or a small pie plate.

3. Smear the fish fillet sticks completely with the mayonnaise, then dip them one by one in the bread-crumb mixture, turning and pressing gently to make an even and thorough coating. Coat each stick on all sides with vegetable oil spray.

4. Set the fish sticks in the basket with at least ¼ inch between them. Air-fry undisturbed for 8 minutes, or until golden brown and crisp.

5. Use a nonstick-safe spatula to gently transfer them from the basket to a wire rack. Cool for only a minute or two before serving.

Crab Stuffed Salmon Roast

Servings: 4

Cooking Time: 20 Minutes

Ingredients:

- 1 (1½-pound) salmon fillet
- salt and freshly ground black pepper
- 6 ounces crabmeat
- 1 teaspoon finely chopped lemon zest
- 1 teaspoon Dijon mustard
- 1 tablespoon chopped fresh parsley, plus more for garnish
- 1 scallion, chopped
- ¼ teaspoon salt
- olive oil

Directions:

1. Prepare the salmon fillet by butterflying it. Slice into the thickest side of the salmon, parallel to the countertop and along the length of the fillet. Don't slice all the way through to the other side – stop about an inch from the edge. Open the salmon up like a book. Season the salmon with salt and freshly ground black pepper.

2. Make the crab filling by combining the crabmeat, lemon zest, mustard, parsley, scallion, salt and freshly ground black pepper in a bowl. Spread this filling in the center of the salmon. Fold one side of the salmon over the filling. Then fold the other side over on top.

3. Transfer the rolled salmon to the center of a piece of parchment paper that is roughly 6- to 7-inches wide and about 12-inches long. The parchment paper will act as a sling, making it easier to put the salmon into the air fryer. Preheat the air fryer to 370°F. Use the parchment paper to transfer the salmon roast to the air fryer basket and tuck the ends of the paper down beside the salmon. Drizzle a little olive oil on top and season with salt and pepper.

4. Air-fry the salmon at 370°F for 20 minutes.

5. Remove the roast from the air fryer and let it rest for a few minutes. Then, slice it, sprinkle some more lemon zest and parsley (or fresh chives) on top and serve.

Fish Tacos With Jalapeño-lime Sauce

Servings: 4   Cooking Time: 7 Minutes

Ingredients:

- Fish Tacos
- 1 pound fish fillets
- ¼ teaspoon cumin
- ¼ teaspoon coriander
- ⅛ teaspoon ground red pepper
- 1 tablespoon lime zest
- ¼ teaspoon smoked paprika
- 1 teaspoon oil
- cooking spray
- 6–8 corn or flour tortillas (6-inch size)

- Jalapeño-Lime Sauce
- ½ cup sour cream
- 1 tablespoon lime juice
- ¼ teaspoon grated lime zest
- ½ teaspoon minced jalapeño (flesh only)
- ¼ teaspoon cumin
- Napa Cabbage Garnish
- 1 cup shredded Napa cabbage
- ¼ cup slivered red or green bell pepper
- ¼ cup slivered onion

Directions:

1. Slice the fish fillets into strips approximately ½-inch thick.

2. Put the strips into a sealable plastic bag along with the cumin, coriander, red pepper, lime zest, smoked paprika, and oil. Massage seasonings into the fish until evenly distributed.

3. Spray air fryer basket with nonstick cooking spray and place seasoned fish inside.

4. Cook at 390°F for approximately 5minutes. Shake basket to distribute fish. Cook an additional 2 minutes, until fish flakes easily.

5. While the fish is cooking, prepare the Jalapeño-Lime Sauce by mixing the sour cream, lime juice, lime zest, jalapeño, and cumin together to make a smooth sauce. Set aside.

6. Mix the cabbage, bell pepper, and onion together and set aside.

7. To warm refrigerated tortillas, wrap in damp paper towels and microwave for 30 to 60 seconds.

8. To serve, spoon some of fish into a warm tortilla. Add one or two tablespoons Napa Cabbage Garnish and drizzle with Jalapeño-Lime Sauce.

Crabmeat-stuffed Flounder

Servings: 3   Cooking Time: 12 Minutes

Ingredients:

- 4½ ounces Purchased backfin or claw crabmeat, picked over for bits of shell and cartilage
- 6 Saltine crackers, crushed into fine crumbs
- 2 tablespoons plus 1 teaspoon Regular or low-fat mayonnaise (not fat-free)
- ¾ teaspoon Yellow prepared mustard
- 1½ teaspoons Worcestershire sauce
- ⅛ teaspoon Celery salt
- 3 5- to 6-ounce skinless flounder fillets
- Vegetable oil spray
- Mild paprika

Directions:

1. Preheat the air fryer to 400°F.

2. Gently mix the crabmeat, crushed saltines, mayonnaise, mustard, Worcestershire sauce, and celery salt in a bowl until well combined.

3. Generously coat the flat side of a fillet with vegetable oil spray. Set the fillet sprayed side down on your work surface. Cut the fillet in half widthwise, then cut one of the halves in half lengthwise. Set a scant ⅓ cup of the crabmeat mixture on top of the undivided half of the fish fillet, mounding the mixture to make an oval that somewhat fits the shape of the fillet with at least a ¼-inch border of fillet beyond the filling all around.

4. Take the two thin divided quarters (that is, the halves of the half) and lay them lengthwise over the filling, overlapping at each end and leaving a little space in the middle where the filling peeks through. Coat the top of the stuffed flounder piece with vegetable oil spray, then sprinkle paprika over the stuffed flounder fillet. Set aside and use the remaining fillet(s) to make more stuffed flounder "packets," repeating steps 3 and

5. Use a nonstick-safe spatula to transfer the stuffed flounder fillets to the basket. Leave as much space between them as possible. Air-fry undisturbed for 12 minutes, or until lightly brown and firm (but not hard).

6. Use that same spatula, plus perhaps another one, to transfer the fillets to a serving platter or plates. Cool for a minute or two, then serve hot.

Shrimp Patties

Servings: 4

Cooking Time: 10 Minutes

Ingredients:

- ½ pound shelled and deveined raw shrimp
- ¼ cup chopped red bell pepper
- ¼ cup chopped green onion
- ¼ cup chopped celery
- 2 cups cooked sushi rice
- ½ teaspoon garlic powder
- ½ teaspoon Old Bay Seasoning
- ½ teaspoon salt
- 2 teaspoons Worcestershire sauce
- ½ cup plain breadcrumbs
- oil for misting or cooking spray

Directions:

1. Finely chop the shrimp. You can do this in a food processor, but it takes only a few pulses. Be careful not to overprocess into mush.

2. Place shrimp in a large bowl and add all other ingredients except the breadcrumbs and oil. Stir until well combined.

3. Preheat air fryer to 390°F.

4. Shape shrimp mixture into 8 patties, no more than ½-inch thick. Roll patties in breadcrumbs and mist with oil or cooking spray.

5. Place 4 shrimp patties in air fryer basket and cook at 390°F for 10 minutes, until shrimp cooks through and outside is crispy.

6. Repeat step 5 to cook remaining shrimp patties.

Lemon-dill Salmon Burgers

Servings: 4

Cooking Time: 8 Minutes

Ingredients:

- 2 (6-ounce) fillets of salmon, finely chopped by hand or in a food processor
- 1 cup fine breadcrumbs
- 1 teaspoon freshly grated lemon zest
- 2 tablespoons chopped fresh dill weed
- 1 teaspoon salt
- freshly ground black pepper
- 2 eggs, lightly beaten
- 4 brioche or hamburger buns
- lettuce, tomato, red onion, avocado, mayonnaise or mustard, to serve

Directions:

1. Preheat the air fryer to 400°F.

2. Combine all the ingredients in a bowl. Mix together well and divide into four balls. Flatten the balls into patties, making an indentation in the center of each patty with your thumb (this will help the burger stay flat as it cooks) and flattening the sides of the burgers so that they fit nicely into the air fryer basket.

3. Transfer the burgers to the air fryer basket and air-fry for 4 minutes. Flip the burgers over and air-fry for another 3 to 4 minutes, until nicely browned and firm to the touch.

4. Serve on soft brioche buns with your choice of topping – lettuce, tomato, red onion, avocado, mayonnaise or mustard.

Tex-mex Fish Tacos

Servings:3

Cooking Time: 7 Minutes

Ingredients:

- ¾ teaspoon Chile powder
- ¼ teaspoon Ground cumin
- ¼ teaspoon Dried oregano
- 3 5-ounce skinless mahi-mahi fillets
- Vegetable oil spray
- 3 Corn or flour tortillas
- 6 tablespoons Diced tomatoes
- 3 tablespoons Regular, low-fat, or fat-free sour cream

Directions:

1. Preheat the air fryer to 400°F.

2. Stir the chile powder, cumin, and oregano in a small bowl until well combined.

3. Coat each piece of fish all over (even the sides and ends) with vegetable oil spray. Sprinkle the spice mixture evenly over all sides of the fillets. Lightly spray them again.

4. When the machine is at temperature, set the fillets in the basket with as much air space between them as possible. Air-fry undisturbed for 7 minutes, until lightly browned and firm but not hard.

5. Use a nonstick-safe spatula to transfer the fillets to a wire rack. Microwave the tortillas on high for a few seconds, until supple. Put a fillet in each tortilla and top each with 2 tablespoons diced tomatoes and 1 tablespoon sour cream.

Horseradish Crusted Salmon

Servings: 2

Cooking Time: 14 Minutes

Ingredients:

- 2 (5-ounce) salmon fillets
- salt and freshly ground black pepper
- 2 teaspoons Dijon mustard
- ½ cup panko breadcrumbs*
- 2 tablespoons prepared horseradish
- ½ teaspoon finely chopped lemon zest
- 1 tablespoon olive oil
- 1 tablespoon chopped fresh parsley

Directions:

1. Preheat the air fryer to 360°F.

2. Season the salmon with salt and freshly ground black pepper. Then spread the Dijon mustard on the salmon, coating the entire surface.

3. Combine the breadcrumbs, horseradish, lemon zest and olive oil in a small bowl. Spread the mixture over the top of the salmon and press down lightly with your hands, adhering it to the salmon using the mustard as "glue".

4. Transfer the salmon to the air fryer basket and air-fry at 360°F for 14 minutes (depending on how thick your fillet is) or until the fish feels firm to the touch. Sprinkle with the parsley.

Sandwiches And Burgers Recipes

Chili Cheese Dogs

Servings: 3

Cooking Time: 12 Minutes

Ingredients:

- ¾ pound Lean ground beef
- 1½ tablespoons Chile powder
- 1 cup plus 2 tablespoons Jarred sofrito
- 3 Hot dogs (gluten-free, if a concern)
- 3 Hot dog buns (gluten-free, if a concern), split open lengthwise
- 3 tablespoons Finely chopped scallion
- 9 tablespoons (a little more than 2 ounces) Shredded Cheddar cheese

Directions:

1. Crumble the ground beef into a medium or large saucepan set over medium heat. Brown well, stirring often to break up the clumps. Add the chile powder and cook for 30 seconds, stirring the whole time. Stir in the sofrito and bring to a simmer. Reduce the heat to low and simmer, stirring occasionally, for 5 minutes. Keep warm.

2. Preheat the air fryer to 400°F.

3. When the machine is at temperature, put the hot dogs in the basket and air-fry undisturbed for 10 minutes, or until the hot dogs are bubbling and blistered, even a little crisp.

4. Use kitchen tongs to put the hot dogs in the buns. Top each with a ½ cup of the ground beef mixture, 1 tablespoon of the minced scallion, and 3 tablespoons of the cheese. (The scallion should go under the cheese so it superheats and wilts a bit.) Set the filled hot dog buns in the basket and air-fry undisturbed for 2 minutes, or until the cheese has melted.

5. Remove the basket from the machine. Cool the chili cheese dogs in the basket for 5 minutes before serving.

Inside-out Cheeseburgers

Servings: 3

Cooking Time: 9-11 Minutes

Ingredients:

- 1 pound 2 ounces 90% lean ground beef
- ¾ teaspoon Dried oregano
- ¾ teaspoon Table salt
- ¾ teaspoon Ground black pepper
- ¼ teaspoon Garlic powder
- 6 tablespoons (about 1½ ounces) Shredded Cheddar, Swiss, or other semi-firm cheese, or a purchased blend of shredded cheeses
- 3 Hamburger buns (gluten-free, if a concern), split open

Directions:

1. Preheat the air fryer to 375°F .

2. Gently mix the ground beef, oregano, salt, pepper, and garlic powder in a bowl until well combined without turning the mixture to mush. Form it into two 6-inch patties for the small batch, three for the medium, or four for the large.

3. Place 2 tablespoons of the shredded cheese in the center of each patty. With clean hands, fold the sides of the patty up to cover the cheese, then pick it up and roll it gently into a ball to seal the cheese inside. Gently press it back into a 5-inch burger without letting any cheese squish out. Continue filling and preparing more burgers, as needed.

4. Place the burgers in the basket in one layer and air-fry undisturbed for 8 minutes for medium or 10 minutes for well-done. (An instant-read meat thermometer won't work for these burgers because it will hit the mostly melted cheese inside and offer a hotter temperature than the surrounding meat.)

5. Use a nonstick-safe spatula, and perhaps a flatware fork for balance, to transfer the burgers to a cutting board. Set the buns cut side down in the basket in one layer (working in batches as necessary) and air-fry undisturbed for 1 minute, to toast a bit and warm up. Cool the burgers a few minutes more, then serve them warm in the buns.

Inside Out Cheeseburgers

Servings: 2

Cooking Time: 20 Minutes

Ingredients:

- ¾ pound lean ground beef
- 3 tablespoons minced onion
- 4 teaspoons ketchup
- 2 teaspoons yellow mustard
- salt and freshly ground black pepper
- 4 slices of Cheddar cheese, broken into smaller pieces
- 8 hamburger dill pickle chips

Directions:

1. Combine the ground beef, minced onion, ketchup, mustard, salt and pepper in a large bowl. Mix well to thoroughly combine the ingredients. Divide the meat into four equal portions.

2. To make the stuffed burgers, flatten each portion of meat into a thin patty. Place 4 pickle chips and half of the cheese onto the center of two of the patties, leaving a rim around the edge of the patty exposed. Place the remaining two patties on top of the first and press the meat together firmly, sealing the edges tightly. With the burgers on a flat surface, press the sides of the burger with the palm of your hand to create a straight edge. This will help keep the stuffing inside the burger while it cooks.

3. Preheat the air fryer to 370°F.

4. Place the burgers inside the air fryer basket and air-fry for 20 minutes, flipping the burgers over halfway through the cooking time.

5. Serve the cheeseburgers on buns with lettuce and tomato.

Black Bean Veggie Burgers

Servings: 3	Cooking Time: 10 Minutes

Ingredients:

- 1 cup Drained and rinsed canned black beans
- ⅓ cup Pecan pieces
- ⅓ cup Rolled oats (not quick-cooking or steel-cut; gluten-free, if a concern)
- 2 tablespoons (or 1 small egg) Pasteurized egg substitute, such as Egg Beaters (gluten-free, if a concern)
- 2 teaspoons Red ketchup-like chili sauce, such as Heinz
- ¼ teaspoon Ground cumin
- ¼ teaspoon Dried oregano
- ¼ teaspoon Table salt
- ¼ teaspoon Ground black pepper
- Olive oil
- Olive oil spray

Directions:

1. Preheat the air fryer to 400°F.
2. Put the beans, pecans, oats, egg substitute or egg, chili sauce, cumin, oregano, salt, and pepper in a food processor. Cover and process to a coarse paste that will hold its shape like sugar-cookie dough, adding olive oil in 1-teaspoon increments to get the mixture to blend smoothly. The amount of olive oil is actually dependent on the internal moisture content of the beans and the oats. Figure on about 1 tablespoon (three 1-teaspoon additions) for the smaller batch, with proportional increases for the other batches. A little too much olive oil can't hurt, but a dry paste will fall apart as it cooks and a far-too-wet paste will stick to the basket.
3. Scrape down and remove the blade. Using clean, wet hands, form the paste into two 4-inch patties for the small batch, three 4-inch patties for the medium, or four 4-inch patties for the large batch, setting them one by one on a cutting board. Generously coat both sides of the patties with olive oil spray.
4. Set them in the basket in one layer. Air-fry undisturbed for 10 minutes, or until lightly browned and crisp at the edges.
5. Use a nonstick-safe spatula, and perhaps a flatware fork for balance, to transfer the burgers to a wire rack. Cool for 5 minutes before serving.

Chicken Saltimbocca Sandwiches

Servings: 3

Cooking Time: 11 Minutes

Ingredients:

- 3 5- to 6-ounce boneless skinless chicken breasts
- 6 Thin prosciutto slices
- 6 Provolone cheese slices
- 3 Long soft rolls, such as hero, hoagie, or Italian sub rolls (gluten-free, if a concern), split open lengthwise
- 3 tablespoons Pesto, purchased or homemade (see the headnote)

Directions:

1. Preheat the air fryer to 400°F.

2. Wrap each chicken breast with 2 prosciutto slices, spiraling the prosciutto around the breast and overlapping the slices a bit to cover the breast. The prosciutto will stick to the chicken more readily than bacon does.

3. When the machine is at temperature, set the wrapped chicken breasts in the basket and air-fry undisturbed for 10 minutes, or until the prosciutto is frizzled and the chicken is cooked through.

4. Overlap 2 cheese slices on each breast. Air-fry undisturbed for 1 minute, or until melted. Take the basket out of the machine.

5. Smear the insides of the rolls with the pesto, then use kitchen tongs to put a wrapped and cheesy chicken breast in each roll.

Reuben Sandwiches

Servings: 2

Cooking Time: 11 Minutes

Ingredients:

- ½ pound Sliced deli corned beef
- 4 teaspoons Regular or low-fat mayonnaise (not fat-free)
- 4 Rye bread slices
- 2 tablespoons plus 2 teaspoons Russian dressing
- ½ cup Purchased sauerkraut, squeezed by the handful over the sink to get rid of excess moisture
- 2 ounces (2 to 4 slices) Swiss cheese slices (optional)

Directions:

1. Set the corned beef in the basket, slip the basket into the machine, and heat the air fryer to 400°F. Air-fry undisturbed for 3 minutes from the time the basket is put in the machine, just to warm up the meat.

2. Use kitchen tongs to transfer the corned beef to a cutting board. Spread 1 teaspoon mayonnaise on one side of each slice of rye bread, rubbing the mayonnaise into the bread with a small flatware knife.

3. Place the bread slices mayonnaise side down on a cutting board. Spread the Russian dressing over the "dry" side of each slice. For one sandwich, top one slice of bread with the corned beef, sauerkraut, and cheese (if using). For two sandwiches, top two slices of bread each with half of the corned beef, sauerkraut, and cheese (if using). Close the sandwiches with the remaining bread, setting it mayonnaise side up on top.

4. Set the sandwich(es) in the basket and air-fry undisturbed for 8 minutes, or until browned and crunchy.

5. Use a nonstick-safe spatula, and perhaps a flatware fork for balance, to transfer the sandwich(es) to a cutting board. Cool for 2 or 3 minutes before slicing in half and serving.

Mexican Cheeseburgers

Servings: 4

Cooking Time: 22 Minutes

Ingredients:

- 1¼ pounds ground beef
- ¼ cup finely chopped onion
- ½ cup crushed yellow corn tortilla chips
- 1 (1.25-ounce) packet taco seasoning
- ¼ cup canned diced green chilies
- 1 egg, lightly beaten
- 4 ounces pepper jack cheese, grated
- 4 (12-inch) flour tortillas
- shredded lettuce, sour cream, guacamole, salsa (for topping)

Directions:

1. Combine the ground beef, minced onion, crushed tortilla chips, taco seasoning, green chilies, and egg in a large bowl. Mix thoroughly until combined – your hands are good tools for this. Divide the meat into four equal portions and shape each portion into an oval-shaped burger.

2. Preheat the air fryer to 370°F.

3. Air-fry the burgers for 18 minutes, turning them over halfway through the cooking time. Divide the cheese between the burgers, lower fryer to 340°F and air-fry for an additional 4 minutes to melt the cheese. (This will give you a burger that is medium-well. If you prefer your cheeseburger medium-rare, shorten the cooking time to about 15 minutes and then add the cheese and proceed with the recipe.)

4. While the burgers are cooking, warm the tortillas wrapped in aluminum foil in a 350°F oven, or in a skillet with a little oil over medium-high heat for a couple of minutes. Keep the tortillas warm until the burgers are ready.

5. To assemble the burgers, spread sour cream over three quarters of the tortillas and top each with some shredded lettuce and salsa. Place the Mexican cheeseburgers on the lettuce and top with guacamole. Fold the tortillas around the burger, starting with the bottom and then folding the sides in over the top. (A little sour cream can help hold the seam of the tortilla together.) Serve immediately.

Turkey Burgers

Servings: 3

Cooking Time: 23 Minutes

Ingredients:

- 1 pound 2 ounces Ground turkey
- 6 tablespoons Frozen chopped spinach, thawed and squeezed dry
- 3 tablespoons Plain panko bread crumbs (gluten-free, if a concern)
- 1 tablespoon Dijon mustard (gluten-free, if a concern)
- 1½ teaspoons Minced garlic
- ¾ teaspoon Table salt
- ¾ teaspoon Ground black pepper
- Olive oil spray
- 3 Kaiser rolls (gluten-free, if a concern), split open

Directions:

1. Preheat the air fryer to 375°F .

2. Gently mix the ground turkey, spinach, bread crumbs, mustard, garlic, salt, and pepper in a large bowl until well combined, trying to keep some of the fibers of the ground turkey intact. Form into two 5-inch-wide patties for the small batch, three 5-inch patties for the medium batch, or four 5-inch patties for the large. Coat each side of the patties with olive oil spray.

3. Set the patties in in the basket in one layer and air-fry undisturbed for 20 minutes, or until an instant-read meat thermometer inserted into the center of a burger registers 165°F. You may need to add 2 minutes to the cooking time if the air fryer is at 360°F.

4. Use a nonstick-safe spatula, and perhaps a flatware fork for balance, to transfer the burgers to a cutting board. Set the buns cut side down in the basket in one layer (working in batches as necessary) and air-fry for 1 minute, to toast a bit and warm up. Serve the burgers warm in the buns.

Eggplant Parmesan Subs

Servings: 2

Cooking Time: 13 Minutes

Ingredients:

- 4 Peeled eggplant slices (about ½ inch thick and 3 inches in diameter)
- Olive oil spray
- 2 tablespoons plus 2 teaspoons Jarred pizza sauce, any variety except creamy
- ¼ cup (about ⅔ ounce) Finely grated Parmesan cheese
- 2 Small, long soft rolls, such as hero, hoagie, or Italian sub rolls (gluten-free, if a concern), split open lengthwise

Directions:

1. Preheat the air fryer to 350°F .

2. When the machine is at temperature, coat both sides of the eggplant slices with olive oil spray. Set them in the basket in one layer and air-fry undisturbed for 10 minutes, until lightly browned and softened.

3. Increase the machine's temperature to 375°F (or 370°F, if that's the closest setting—unless the machine is already at 360°F, in which case leave it alone). Top each eggplant slice with 2 teaspoons pizza sauce, then 1 tablespoon cheese. Air-fry undisturbed for 2 minutes, or until the cheese has melted.

4. Use a nonstick-safe spatula, and perhaps a flatware fork for balance, to transfer the eggplant slices cheese side up to a cutting board. Set the roll(s) cut side down in the basket in one layer (working in batches as necessary) and air-fry undisturbed for 1 minute, to toast the rolls a bit and warm them up. Set 2 eggplant slices in each warm roll.

Printed by Libri Plureos GmbH in Hamburg,
Germany